Sunlight in December

Sunlight in December

*A Mother's Story
of Finding the
Goodness of God
in the Storm of Grief*

KRISTIN HERNANDEZ

LUMINARE PRESS
WWW.LUMINAREPRESS.COM

SUNLIGHT IN DECEMBER: A Mother's Story of Finding the Goodness of
God in the Storm of Grief
Copyright © 2021 by Kristin Hernandez

Scripture quotations are from the ESV® Bible (The Holy Bible, English
Standard Version®), copyright © 2001 by Crossway, a publishing ministry
of Good News Publishers. Used by permission. All rights reserved.

Cover Photo by Gretchen Seelenbinder on Unsplash.com
Author photograph by Veronica Gutierrez

Printed in the United States of America

Luminare Press
442 Charnelton St.
Eugene, OR 97401
www.luminarepress.com

LCCN: 2021911738
ISBN: 978-1-64388-725-8

To my **Grieving Together** *sisters, who walked beside me in our earliest days of grief and pointed me to the Light.*

Contents

One

Blessed are those

I have always loved the way rays of sunlight peek through the clouds after a rainstorm. Because I grew up in the desert of Southern California, rain has always been a novelty in my life. But when it did come, I always looked forward to the spectacular view after the storm. The way the rays of sunlight burst through the dark clouds and shine upon the earth brings me to a place of awe and wonder. It looks as if the heavens have opened and as if love and warmth are pouring down. It is a reminder that the sun was always there, even as the rains plummeted down upon the earth, bringing thunder and flash flood warnings with it. A calm after the storm. To me, it looks like hope.

The winter of 2015 felt especially cold to me. I don't remember the temperatures, the weather, or many of the details surrounding the holidays that year. Looking back, most of that season is blurry and hard to recall. I certainly remember the cold, though. It wasn't a physical coolness, but rather a sort of winter inside of me. Things felt cold. The sky looked cold. The world felt cold.

The trees were finally stripped bare after weeks of their leaves drifting to the ground like my tears. Questions, confusion, and defeat whirled around me like harsh winter winds as I struggled to stand beneath the force of it all.

Yet even in the coldest winter, the sun continued to rise each day and warm the earth. Rays of sunlight stretched across the sky each morning and served as a reminder of God's continual grace and mercy in my life. Like sunlight, it pierced through my cold and darkness daily, despite the bitterness of winter.

Even when the storm rages on, the sun will shine again. Even when the winds howl, the earth is barren, and the world feels so cold, the sun continues to shine. There is still sunlight in December. There is joy coming. There is hope because of Christ.

When our hearts feel heavy, when the worries of the world try to hijack our hearts, when we feel empty and barren, the joy of the Lord can pierce through the darkness. The Light shines in the darkness and the darkness has not overcome it (John 1:5).

When I was in college, I started a blog called *Sunshine in December*. I was writing for my university newspaper and the blog began as a news writing class assignment. I picked the name on a whim. I love summer sunshine, December is my birth month, and it sounded hopeful. At the time, I had no idea how fitting the name would prove to be when I returned to blogging several years later. In that time, the "Sunshine in December" domain name was snatched up, but I began writing under *Sunlight in December*.

After high school, I headed off to a four-year Christian university where I met my husband, Chris, during the spring semester of my freshman year. We had enrolled into the same philosophy class and easily formed a friendship after we had been placed in the same discussion group. A romantic relationship was the last thing on my mind, but the more time I spent with Chris, the more my attraction toward him grew. From our first conversation, I was immediately captivated by Chris's love for Christ and his compassion for others. He was exactly what I was looking for in a guy. Our friendship grew over the summer and we went on our first official date the following September. The rest is history. When I was twenty-two, I graduated college with an engagement ring on my finger and we were married the following fall. We moved into a cute one-bedroom apartment a few blocks from our alma mater, where I had been offered a job on campus. We were happily married, working in stable jobs, serving in our church, and involved in our community. Parenthood would surely be the next step for us. That's how it works, right? Take the right steps, reap the blessings. At least that's what I thought at the time.

What does it even mean to be "blessed"? Growing up in the American church, I often heard Christians call themselves "blessed" when life was filled with laughter, comfort, and security. If I asked someone how they were doing, they frequently responded with "blessed"—"blessed to have this job," "blessed to have my family," or "blessed to be healthy." The word "blessing" was often used as if it were synonymous with "prosperous" and I never questioned that. It made sense to me. I had a happy childhood, I had a loving family, and I always felt safe. My life felt pretty good and I certainly would have called it "blessed."

I have wrestled with the meaning of this word over the years. There was a time when I subconsciously believed blessings were contingent on my external circumstances. The belief was subtle. If you would have asked me what it meant to be blessed, I probably would have told you it was much deeper than our health or our security. I knew this in my head, but my emotions and my actions weren't lining up with what I knew to be true. It wasn't until I encountered intense pain that I began to consider what it truly means to be blessed. It was in that season that the word "blessed" began to grate on me. If I'm being completely honest, I should say I wanted to roll my eyes at anyone who used that word.

The world that had once felt so safe suddenly felt broken. The more suffering I experienced, the more I noticed the incredible pain of those around me. I thought about my Christian brothers and sisters living in extreme pain, sickness, or poverty. I cried with a dear friend when her husband insisted on divorce. I watched my mother undergo surgeries to remove thyroid cancer. I sat with a young man who had lost his entire family during the Rwandan genocide. I wept in a hospital room and held my newborn son as his organs failed and his body grew cold. Were we any less blessed than our brothers and sisters who were living in peace?

I knew that couldn't be true. I marveled at the peace I saw in their tear-filled eyes. I wondered at the joy they had after walking through such trials. While their circumstances were certainly far from "prosperous," anyone who met them could not deny they were blessed.

There was a time when I felt as if the word "blessed" was overused in Christian circles, but I've changed my mind. I believe it is underused. We don't say it enough. It is easy for us to shout it from the rooftops when we receive a promotion, welcome a new baby, or achieve a lifelong goal. It is easy for us to declare God's goodness when He restores a friendship, provides a new home, or heals us from cancer.

And we certainly *should* praise Him for these good gifts. Every good thing in our life is a blessing from God (James 1:17) and we are right to give Him glory for every happiness and each answered prayer.

But this is only a small part of a much bigger picture. With Christ, we are blessed in the midst of sorrow, rejection, and loss. We are blessed when we are overlooked for a promotion. We are blessed when a close friend betrays us. We are blessed when the cancer becomes terminal.

Jesus gives us a much more complete definition of what it truly means to be blessed in Matthew 5:3–12, and it's unlike what I had subconsciously come to believe. He says:

> Blessed are the poor in spirit, for theirs is the kingdom of heaven. Blessed are those who mourn, for they shall be comforted. Blessed are the meek, for they shall inherit the earth. Blessed are those who hunger and thirst for righteousness, for they shall be satisfied. Blessed are the merciful, for they shall receive mercy. Blessed are the pure in heart, for they shall see God. Blessed are the peacemakers, for they shall be called sons of God. Blessed are those who are persecuted for righteousness' sake, for theirs is the kingdom of heaven. Blessed are you when others revile you and persecute you and utter all kinds of evil against you falsely on my account. Rejoice and be glad, for your reward is great in heaven, for so they persecuted the prophets who were before you. (Matthew 5:3–12)

Poor in spirit. Those who mourn. Those who are persecuted, insulted, and rejected for Christ.

In seasons of pain, it is tempting for me to feel less than or to ask what I've done wrong. Many of us may have found ourselves in this position, wondering if those who are mourning are being robbed of God's blessing. I love how Jesus shatters that assumption. He calls them blessed. He calls the weary and gives them rest (Matthew 11:28).

We can have access to the greatest blessing of all—Christ. Through Christ we have access to every spiritual blessing (Ephesians 1). We know our suffering is not the end of the story. We can praise Him and declare "I am blessed" with the same confidence in seasons of grief, poverty, and death as we do in seasons of joy, abundance, and life. In sunshine and in torrential rain.

I have wanted to be a mother for as long as I can remember. As a little girl, I often dreamed of getting married, settling into a comfortable house, and spending my days holding babies and kissing scraped knees. It seemed like a simple dream. In my youthful innocence, I never considered our plans for parenthood might not unfold as effortlessly as I had imagined.

For three years, Chris and I struggled to conceive. All of my blood tests had returned normal and there was no apparent explanation as to why a healthy twenty-five-year-old woman should have absent menstrual cycles. Doctors told us we would likely need to go through fertility treatments if we wanted to pursue pregnancy.

I was crushed. In my mind, motherhood was the natural next step following marriage. Our marriage was happy, our jobs were going well, and we had recently bought our first house. I felt as if we had done all the "right things" and I never saw this challenge coming. The road toward fertility treatments seemed long, daunting, and expensive.

Seeing my distress (and trusting God's timing much more than I did), Chris gently suggested we take a few months to rest after a long season of blood tests and ultrasounds. There was no need to schedule the consultation with the infertility specialist right away and my weary heart welcomed the break.

We never made it to that first appointment.

In February 2015, I came down with what I thought was the flu and I just couldn't seem to shake it. After a few weeks of seeing me struggle with low energy and constant queasiness, Chris said the words that would eventually change everything.

"Baby, I think you should take a pregnancy test," he suggested. "What if you're pregnant?"

I scoffed, practically spewing the water I had just sipped out of my mouth. "I'm *not* pregnant," I said abruptly. Honestly, I was a bit angry he would even suggest the possibility of a pregnancy. He knew just how many tears I had cried over negative pregnancy tests and frustrating medical appointments. He knew how many times my veins had been poked to draw blood and how few answers we had received. He had stood beside me for the past few years. He knew we couldn't get pregnant.

"You *know* I can't get pregnant," I added adamantly.

Chris, patient and unwavering as ever, just offered me a gentle smile. "We don't know that for sure," he said.

I was not amused by his optimism. "Fine," I said with a shrug. "If I'm not feeling better in a few days, I'll take a pregnancy test. I promise." I was confident my queasiness would subside soon and the whole ordeal would be over.

I remembered my promise two days later–on March 10, 2015. Chris had just left for work and I had a few days off for spring break. I sleepily stumbled out of bed and grabbed a pregnancy test on my way to the bathroom.

My emotions surrounding this pregnancy test were so different than they had been in the past. I should say they were nearly nonexistent. I wasn't on the edge of my seat and my heart wasn't racing. It was one of the calmest, most nonchalant pregnancy test experiences you can imagine. Years of medical appointments, blood tests, and absent menstrual cycles had caused the turbulent emotions I felt with each pregnancy test to fizzle out into a flat line. On this day, I expected nothing.

A few minutes later I picked up the test to view the results. I gasped. This was the last thing I expected. There were two pink lines. I had never seen *two* pink lines before. Grabbing the instructions, I held them close to my face to examine what a positive test looked like. My eyes scanned back and forth between the test and the diagram for a minute; I was unable to believe what I was seeing. They were identical.

I still didn't believe it could be true and I immediately drove to Target to purchase a fancy digital pregnancy test. I figured a test that says either "PREGNANT" or "NOT PREGNANT" would be foolproof. A few hours later I stared at the fancy test, which displayed the word "PREG-NANT" on the screen. I was finally convinced. My hands trembled and I immediately sank to the floor, bursting into deep sobs of gratitude.

My mind flashed back to the countless blood tests, doctor visits, and tears I had endured over the previous few years. I felt the weight of the countless times I had slipped into the bathroom to cry after yet another woman announced her pregnancy. I remembered the countless times I had smiled and desperately tried to brush it off when someone had innocently asked me when my husband and I wanted to start a family. I felt the weight and reverence that comes with years of waiting and yearning for a child. I couldn't help but cry tears of immense joy and gratitude. Our dream was coming true without any interventions, when doctors told me it may never be possible.

We were pregnant.

Chris and I were completely overwhelmed with gratitude to God for this incredible gift. For years, we had prayed God would give us a child. We had prayed for His timing. We had prayed for a miracle. After years of prayer, He had said yes. We were finally pregnant, at a time when we had least expected it.

The first trimester of pregnancy wasn't easy. Twice we rushed to the hospital after I noticed blood in my underwear. Twice we thought we were miscarrying our miracle baby. Twice the bleeding stopped and our baby continued to grow. Twice God had intervened when all seemed hopeless. I knew He had a plan for our child and for our family. I confidently praised God for this miracle.

I had no idea the next few months would contain a series of faith-building trials and joys and that God, Who holds all things together, would bring comfort in the midst of unthinkable pain. That He would remain both powerful and good in the months to come, even when I wanted to run away. That this blessing would come in ways I didn't expect. I had no idea this was only the beginning of the story.

Two

The anomaly

I loved being pregnant. I constantly felt giddy (and nauseous) and savored each moment. I dreamed of the future and read every pregnancy book or article I could get my hands on. We took a photo of my expanding belly each Saturday to capture physical memories of the growth. Chris and I dreamed of who our little one would be, what he or she would look like, and what life would be like for our growing family. Our home was filled with lots of laughter. Everything felt perfect.

I felt my first flutter when I was about twelve weeks pregnant. I had read that most women don't feel movement until further along, but my confidence in what I had felt was only confirmed as time passed and the flutters grew into kicks. Our active baby regularly danced in my belly.

I knew hardly anything about this growing child, but it didn't matter—the love I felt was strong and unconditional. The gratitude I felt over this new life inside of me had been intensified by years of longing. Our bond grew stronger each day.

Chris and I were counting down to our twenty-week anatomy scan where we would learn if our baby was a boy or a girl. We didn't have a preference on the sex, but we wanted to know as much as we could about our baby. We couldn't wait to tell our families, discuss names, and decorate the nursery. I was aware this mid-pregnancy ultrasound was conducted to check on the baby's development, but I wasn't worried about health. It never crossed my mind that anything could be wrong. Our little one constantly fluttered inside of me, reminding me he or she was strong and active. Certainly our long-awaited miracle child was healthy. Besides, I had been doing everything "right." I never missed one day of my prenatal vitamins. I ate healthy foods and made sure our baby was getting the perfect balance of nutrients. I forced myself to eat healthy meals when I felt nauseous. I drank plenty of water. I never once touched caffeine, deli meats, soft cheeses, or raw sushi, and I rarely consumed refined flour or sugar. I stayed active and kept up with a doctor-approved exercise routine. I slept soundly at night and even managed to squeeze in naps when I felt tired. I was extremely rigid and took pride in my pursuit of "pregnancy perfectionism." I felt energized and amazing, thus I was confident our baby felt the same.

The day of the anatomy scan finally came and I could barely contain my excitement. This was the day the long-anticipated secret would finally be revealed. When we stopped for lunch on our way to the appointment, I strategically ordered a salad loaded with fruit and honey sesame dressing in hopes the natural sugars would make the baby active enough to get a good view of his or her anatomy.

At the hospital, Chris was instructed to wait in the lobby while I was escorted back into the examination room for an ultrasound. He would be able to join me again at the end of the exam.

The ultrasound technician squeezed warm gel onto my belly and began to examine our sweet little baby. The screen was turned away from me and toward her, so I could not see much. I was not worried. I closed my eyes and daydreamed about our little boy or girl.

A smile spread across the technician's face and her eyes opened wide with surprise. "Oh my goodness!" she exclaimed. "Your baby just did a full somersault. It used both feet to push off the side of your uterus and do a full flip!"

I chuckled and told her how active our baby had been over the past few weeks. As she continued to study the screen and take measurements, I closed my eyes and day-dreamed about our energetic child. *Will he or she play sports? How about Chris's sense of humor?*

"Alright, we're almost done," the technician said. "You can go and get your husband from the waiting room and we can give him a look. I'm going to step out for a minute and I'll meet you both back here."

I pulled my shirt back down over my abdomen and peeked out into the waiting room. I caught Chris's gaze and motioned for him to come with me. I took a seat back on the reclining table and Chris sat in a chair near my head. I told him about our baby's daredevil tactics and impressive flips. We sat alone in the quiet room for about fifteen minutes before the technician finally returned. When she returned, she seemed to speak more directly and with less emotion than she had before. It had been an hour since the exam had started and I assumed she was simply getting down to business so she could continue with her schedule. In hindsight, I can see her sudden abruptness was caused by more than met the eye.

"Alright, you both want to know the gender, right?"

Chris and I both nodded. This is what we had been waiting for.

"Looks like a boy," she said matter-of-factly. She pointed out the determining factor. "See?" We were ecstatic. For some reason (you could call it some sort of mistaken intuition), we had both always envisioned us having daughters, but we could not be happier to be expecting a son.

"So everything looks good with him?" Chris asked.

"I just take the photos," the tech said. "Your doctor will call you if they see any concerns." With that we left, confident everything was perfect.

We couldn't wait to tell our families. We had plans to drive to Las Vegas the following Monday for a family reunion with Chris's side of the family. Family from Southern California and North Carolina would all be together for the first time in several years and it would be the perfect occasion to make the big announcement.

Early Monday morning, Chris and I began the four-hour drive from our home in California to Las Vegas, Nevada. Our out-of-state family had flown into Las Vegas that morning and we had arranged to meet for lunch as soon as we arrived. After a few hours of driving through the desert, I saw the skyline of the Las Vegas Strip pop up on the horizon. I couldn't wait to get out of the car and stretch my legs.

If you've been to Las Vegas, you know it's typically warm year round, but during the summer months you can usually expect temperatures above 100 degrees Fahrenheit. I can clearly remember the dry, intense heat that met us as we parked in front of the restaurant and began to step out of the car. The details of that moment are still so vivid.

As I stepped out of the car and into the scorching heat, my cell phone rang. I was surprised to see the number for our hospital scroll across the screen. I was up to date on my appointments and couldn't think of any reason for them to be calling me.

I answered the phone as I stepped out of the car and closed the car door behind me. "Hello?"

It was a receptionist from the hospital. "Hi, Kristin. We were wondering if you are available to come in tomorrow at 9:00 a.m. for an appointment."

I was confused. My next few appointments had already been set up with my ob-gyn. "I'm actually on vacation right now," I said. "Is there another time that would be okay? I'll be back next week."

"Well," the receptionist sounded slightly hesitant. "If you can't come in any sooner, we can certainly make an appointment for next week. You'll actually have two appointments, but we can schedule them for the same day. The first appointment will be with our genetic counselor and the second will be to conduct a level II ultrasound with a perinatologist…"

I froze. The words "genetic counselor" and "perinatologist" flashed in my head like bright red warning signs. I grabbed Chris's hand as he walked toward the restaurant, signaling him that this was an important call and I needed him to wait outside with me.

He caught on and looked concerned. "Can I ask what this is about?" I asked. "Is something wrong?"

"We just need to discuss some things from your recent ultrasound. I do not have any details to share with you, but the counselor and the doctor will be able to tell you more when they see you," she said kindly. "We can get you in next Monday, one week from today."

"Um…okay. Okay, that's fine. I can do Monday." The call ended and I immediately broke down sobbing. I relayed the information to Chris as we stood in the hot parking lot. I was so worried about our baby.

What is going on with our baby? What if he is in danger? Something must be wrong with him. Why wouldn't they tell us anything more over the phone? Oh God, please help us.

By now, the restaurant was filled with family. Aunts, uncles, and cousins exchanged warm hugs and excited chatter filled the room. I just couldn't engage in the festivities. I had entered the restaurant with tears streaking down my face and the inability to squeak out a word without breaking down. Chris encouraged me to eat half of a chicken wrap and assured me it was okay to cry. I ate in silence, surrounded by the sounds of laughter. It all felt so strange and uncomfortable.

After lunch, we all checked in to the hotel and agreed to meet again in two hours to set out to see the sights. Chris and I finally took a moment to process in the silence of our hotel room.

"If you think we should leave, I'm willing to drive home," Chris said, sitting next to me on the edge of the bed. We discussed our options and our fears. Chris suggested I call back to see if we could gather any additional details that could be helpful in making a decision. I called the receptionist and told her we were willing to come home the next day if the appointment was urgent. The friendly receptionist tried her best to provide answers, but wasn't able to share many details over the phone. "I'm going to walk down to the doctor's office and personally find out for you," she offered. "I'll give you a call back in ten minutes."

My phone rang exactly ten minutes later. The doctor had recommended we come home and have our appointment as soon as possible, as long as it was not a major inconvenience for us. We set our appointment for the following morning at 9:00.

I wanted to go home immediately and Chris wanted to stay and spend the rest of the day with family. I considered his point of view and knew it made sense to stay a little longer. There was no reason to leave immediately, as it was only 1:00 in the afternoon and our appointment was not until the next morning. We had already driven this far and were with family we had not seen in two years. We made the decision to attempt to relax and enjoy the afternoon before making the long drive home that evening.

It made no difference to me. Whether at home or walking down the Las Vegas Strip, all I could think about was our baby. I couldn't shake the dark cloud looming over us. The laughter and the smiles around me seemed out of place.

We told our family as much as we knew and were met with understanding and support. We decided to drive back to California after dinner. I collapsed into bed as soon as we arrived home and struggled to sleep. Even in the comfort of our own bed, sleep seemed like an impossible goal. I couldn't rein in my turbulent thoughts. I tossed and turned while considering every possibility. I just wanted to have answers so we could move forward.

"I hope it's me," I told Chris, as we drove to the hospital the next morning. "I hope something is wrong with me. Maybe they noticed a tumor on the ultrasound. Maybe I have some sort of condition that could take my life during childbirth. It should be me. I'd take any news about my own health over negative news about his."

It was at this moment that I realized the depth and the intensity of a mother's love. There was no doubt in my mind I would do anything to save our son. I would give my life for him. For the first time it really hit me. No matter what events would follow, I was and always would be a mom.

Upon arriving at the hospital we were called into the genetic counselor's office. I looked around the room and felt like it was purposefully designed to soften the blow of bad news. It didn't work—I felt sick to my stomach. Natural light poured through the window. A large bookshelf displayed various reading materials and lovely decorations. We sat in two padded chairs across from the counselor's wooden desk. A box of tissues was strategically placed in front of us, ready to collect the waterfall of tears about to flow.

The genetic counselor introduced herself to us. I immediately noticed her gentle, motherly demeanor. Despite her kindness, I had never felt more fearful in my life. "Did either of you have any questions for me?" she asked, as she took a seat at her desk.

What in the world is going on? What's happening to our baby? Why are we here?

Chris and I exchanged a confused look. We did not know where to begin. We did not know the nature of the appointment and we could not think of specific questions to ask. We had no specific questions, yet the entire situation felt like one tremendous question.

Chris broke the silence. "We don't know why we are here," he told her. "All we know is it was strongly recommended for us to come in today and we are assuming it has something to do with the ultrasound we had last week."

"Okay, we should start from the beginning," the geneticist said. She opened a file on her computer and turned the screen toward us. In gentle tones, she explained a small piece of our baby's brain was missing. Not only this, but our baby boy also had hydrocephalus, which is just a fancy word to describe a buildup of fluid on the brain. The missing piece of his brain resembled a condition called Dandy Walker syndrome. The condition affects individuals in a variety of ways, ranging from unnoticeable to severe. It would be difficult to determine the extent of the physical and mental challenges our baby might face until after he was born.

Just as the information began to sink in, the genetic counselor delivered more news. She explained the doctor was not able to locate several components of our baby's heart in the ultrasound photos, which is why we needed to meet with the perinatologist for the level II ultrasound. "It's possible the ultrasound technician simply wasn't able to get a clear picture," she added. "The perinatologist will be able to explain what she is looking at in real time."

My brain felt like it was going to explode as I tried to listen to her describe more details about our son's condition and our next steps. The words jumbled together and I could not focus. I couldn't think straight and I felt like I was drowning, thrashing to keep my head above the waves. *Something is wrong with our baby. Our baby is in danger. Oh Lord, please save him. Please wake me up from this nightmare.*

The genetic counselor explained we could opt in to receive a test called an amniocentesis. In this procedure, a long needle is inserted into the uterus through the mother's abdominal wall to collect a sample of amniotic fluid. The fluid contains fetal tissue, which is tested for chromosomal abnormalities. "The test also comes with a small risk of miscarriage or stillbirth," she explained. "Unfortunately, having a baby with abnormalities already puts you at a higher risk."

"Would it help us to know a specific diagnosis ahead of time? Would these test results help the hospital to provide the best medical care for him?" I asked.

"Not exactly," she said. "The test will help you both prepare for the future and will give you a better picture of what to expect. There is not much else it will do for him, but sometimes it is nice to know exactly what is going on so you can prepare."

"Can we do the same testing after he's born?" I asked. "Is there any reason we'd need to do it now?"

"We can collect a sample of blood from the umbilical cord after he is born, if he survives delivery. If he dies in the womb, we may not be able to collect the cells we need."

He could die? How serious is this?

We felt conflicted. While it would be nice to have a specific diagnosis, we did not want to put our son at a higher risk for stillbirth. The counselor seemed to notice our confusion and distress. "You do not need to decide right away," she assured us. Her voice remained soft and kind. "Just keep in mind it could take three weeks for test results to come back. If you want to keep your options open, you may want to make a decision sooner."

I didn't understand what she meant. "Options?"

"Yes, you're already twenty weeks pregnant and you're nearing the twenty-four week termination deadline," she explained.

I felt like someone had kicked me in the gut. The overwhelming urge to protect our child surged in me. Having a child with special needs was never on our radar, but we were more than willing to take on the challenge and to love him regardless of the prognosis. I struggled to find the words to say.

Many words jumbled through my brain, but when I opened my mouth, the only words I could utter were, "He kicks me every day. He moves so much."

"We will love him and care for him no matter what his circumstances are," Chris added, giving a much clearer account of what I was trying to say. Tears were streaming from my eyes. I was not sure when I had started crying, but I could tell I had already been crying for a while. "We definitely want this baby," I added, finally collecting myself enough to formulate my thoughts into a complete sentence.

The geneticist nodded and offered a soft smile, receiving the desperate message we were trying to convey. "The next step would be to meet with the perinatologist," she explained. "If you'd like, I can see if she is able to meet with you now so you do not need to wait an hour for your scheduled appointment. You can wait in my office while I go check."

As she closed the door, I fell onto Chris's shoulder and allowed the tears to completely take over. Chris put his arm around me and stroked my hair as I buried my face into his shoulder and sobbed. I wasn't ashamed of my loud wailing and endless tears. I felt I had every right to cry. I could tell Chris was incredibly concerned, but he was doing his very best to be calm for me. His arm felt strong around me and I found comfort knowing we would face this together.

The counselor returned and told us the perinatologist had a cancellation and was available to meet with us immediately. I was very thankful she was able to see us early. The last thing I wanted was to return to the waiting room where dozens of happy couples were waiting for their routine prenatal checkups.

The geneticist led us to an examination room, where a nurse checked my vitals and told us the perinatologist would be with us soon. I sat on the edge of the examination table, trying to stop the tears from flowing. Chris solemnly sat in a chair beside me and took my hand.

"Should we get the test?" I asked after we were alone. "I don't want to hurt him. I want to know what's wrong, but I wouldn't be able to live with myself if something happened to him."

"It didn't seem like the results would change anything," Chris said. "The genetic counselor made it sound like the doctors would give him the same care regardless. And we could still do the test after he is born."

"Yeah, I think we should wait. You?"

Chris nodded solemnly. "Yeah, let's wait." Decision made.

A petite woman with a kind smile entered the room and introduced herself as our perinatologist. Her demeanor immediately put our anxious hearts at ease. She was direct yet compassionate. We needed someone like her—someone who would cut to the chase and give us the truth, but who genuinely cared about our turbulent emotions and our child's health. She explained she was going to do an ultrasound to confirm or disprove any findings from the original exam. She explained photos do not always capture a complete look and she wanted to do a live exam to see our baby in real time. "The doctor who examined your ultrasound photos noticed several abnormalities and I want to take a closer look to see how your baby is doing," she said. There was a gentleness in her voice and she seemed to genuinely care about us and about our son.

I leaned back on the exam table and she began to examine our baby via ultrasound. She moved the ultrasound probe across my belly and leaned close to the monitor. Her forehead wrinkled as she focused on the screen. The silence was deafening.

She turned the screen toward us and zoomed in on our son's brain. "Do you see this right here?" she asked, pointing to the back of his head. I focused on the black-and-white image and squinted to get a better look. I was not quite sure what we were looking at, but I did notice a small section at the back of his head was a different shade of grey.

"There seems to be extra spacing at the back of his head. It looks like he is missing a piece of his cerebellum called the vermis. There are also extra pockets of fluid in a few places on the brain. I'll keep a close eye on this over the coming months. We do not want the fluid to expand." She saved dozens of images and recorded measurements of our baby's brain.

Next she shifted her focus to his heart. She told us the heart was much larger than average and was shaped abnormally. One of the walls of his heart was larger and seemed to be covered with extra muscle, which is often a sign that particular section of the heart is working hard to keep up with normal demands. "It's like any muscle you exercise," she explained. "The harder you work it, the bigger it gets. This section appears to be working harder than normal."

His brain and his heart weren't the only concerns. Our baby's stomach was in the center of his body, whereas most stomachs are on the left. His chin seemed to be smaller than normal. He was growing slower than the average rate.

"With all of these abnormalities, it's very possible there is some sort of genetic anomaly," she said directly yet kindheartedly. "No particular syndrome comes to mind when I look at him. It's probably something rare and probably a random occurrence.

"There is nothing you could have done to prevent this. These anomalies were probably in the works by the time you had your first positive pregnancy test."

Hot tears had been dripping down my face throughout the entire visit. I could not believe this was happening to us. To our sweet baby. Our miracle. I would have done anything to trade places with him.

"There is a possibility this baby could have severe disabilities," she said softly. "Do you both have a good support system? It's going to take a village to care for him. Are you prepared to have a child with special needs?"

The question was asked with the utmost care, but it struck me as odd. We definitely were not prepared, but that never felt like a prerequisite to me. Is anyone ever prepared for something like this? Is anyone ever prepared to become a parent at all? What could possibly prepare us for this?

"We're willing to prepare ourselves for whatever happens," I said. "We're prepared to love him no matter what."

Chris took my hand and nodded. "We'll do whatever we need to protect him," he added.

Our next step would be to meet with a pediatric cardiologist and another perinatologist in Los Angeles. "I am going to make a referral for you today. The pediatric cardiologist specializes in infant hearts and he will be able to give you a much clearer idea of what is going on. There is also the possibility the L.A. medical team will want you to deliver there. I am going to let him make that decision when you meet.

"Until then, you'll continue to meet with me every two weeks. We'll check on your baby's growth and his well-being each time we meet. Starting at thirty weeks, you'll come in once a week and we'll observe him for thirty minutes at each time. Be ready. If at any point after thirty weeks he seems like he is struggling, we may choose to deliver him so we can help him."

Our perinatologist gave us a reassuring smile and called us brave. She was genuine, but the compliment felt difficult to accept. I felt anything but brave. I was just a mama fighting for her child and I was scared.

I felt numb as we walked back to the car. The tears had not stopped falling since the day before and I felt exhausted. I did not want to talk to anyone. I did not want to see anyone. I did not even want to go home. Chris put his arms around me and pulled me close. I sank against his chest. I just wanted to cry. The helplessness I felt was overwhelming.

A chapter of my life closed that day. The naïve girl who believed "good people" would have lives filled with ease, comfort, and prosperity died sitting in the genetic counselor's padded chair. I was no longer the optimistic girl who lived in a world where innocent babies don't get sick. I felt as if I had entered the week as a vibrant, hopeful twentysomething, and had stepped out as a worn, tired woman who had seen a glimpse of the battlefield ahead and the trauma that would likely come with it. June 23, 2015, was a defining day that split my life into two chapters: before when life felt so simple, and after when I learned some babies have to fight to live even before they are born.

After much discussion, Chris and I decided to drive back to Las Vegas and rejoin Chris's family for the remainder of the reunion. Our perinatologist had encouraged us to continue with our normal routine and to try to take our minds off our worry by doing something fun. Everything sounded like a horrible idea. Taking in the bright lights and sounds of Vegas sounded miserable. Sitting in our quiet home and crying sounded miserable. Nothing sounded fun or restful. I didn't want to do anything. I only wanted this nightmare to end.

I hit my breaking point on the four-hour drive back to Las Vegas. I was convinced my eyes could not possibly have any tears left, but I was wrong. I choked and gasped for breath as the sobs racked my body.

"Talk to me," Chris said softly, taking my hand.

"Why is this happening?" I cried loudly. "Why? It's not fair! Why would God allow this to happen to us? After everything we went through? We couldn't get pregnant for so long! We prayed so hard for a baby! And now this? It's not fair!"

I began to scream at the heavens. My voice rose with each statement. "Where are you, God? We did everything right! We love each other, we have jobs, we can give him a good life! We love him! We prayed for so long! Why do people who are trying to avoid pregnancy get pregnant so easily? People who don't want their kids? I hate this! How is any of this fair? Why would you do this to us?" I coughed and gasped for air, my face soaked with tears. My body crumpled onto the center console and Chris rubbed my back, eyes still fixed on the road.

"I know, baby, I know," he said. "None of it is fair. But I know God has a plan. I know he does."

I knew he was speaking truth, but surrender is often much easier said than done. I knew God is sovereign over life and I am unworthy to claim the "right" to a healthy child. Who was I to claim I had been "good enough" to earn anything at all? If we could simply "earn" good things, why would Jesus have needed to come to earth? Wasn't this the point of His death on the cross? To die in our place so we would not need to earn His forgiveness? I took a deep breath and tried to swallow the bitterness that had welled up in me. Deep down, I knew I was no better than the "undeserving" parents I had shaken my fist at.

Chris and I began to pray. We prayed God would use our baby in big ways. We prayed He would give us peace and comfort. We asked that He would provide complete healing over this miracle baby.

Somewhere before the Nevada border I volunteered to drive. Chris had made the drive to and from Las Vegas the day before and I could tell he was weary. I did not mind driving and I welcomed the opportunity for a distraction.

My phone vibrated. One of my friends had sent me a Facebook message with a link to a devotional she had read earlier that week. I asked Chris if he would read it aloud. The devotional explained how God allows trials in our lives to strengthen us and to give us joy. It compared our trials with ravenous wolves set free to help manage a deer population overrunning a particular region. Once the deer population drops, the plants begin to grow again and positively impact the area's waterways. What once looked like devastation helps the region thrive and return to its fruitful state. The devotion ended with James 1:2–4: "Count it all joy, my brothers, when you meet trials of various kinds for you know that the testing of your faith produces steadfastness. And let steadfastness have its full effect, that you may be perfect and complete, lacking in nothing."

Chris finished reading and immediately went silent. I tried to stay focused on the road, but I saw his body crumple out of the corner of my eye. He bent over and rested his head on his knees. I reached over and rested my hand on his shoulder. I felt his body shudder and he let out a cry.

"It just all really hit me," he said through tears. Chris has a soft heart, but he does not cry often. I wished I was not driving so I could wrap both of my arms around him.

Tears filled my eyes and I cried with him. I wished I could say or do more to help him. Once again I felt so helpless.

We crossed the Nevada border, both crying over our sick baby and over the puzzling goodness of our perfect God.

Three

Strong, safe, and enduring

C hris and I had settled on two baby names we loved. Ironically, both were girl names.

A week before finding out our baby's sex, Chris and I had spent the evening in Laguna Beach recreating our first date. We grabbed a pizza at BJ's and watched the sun set into the Pacific. As we drove home, we discussed baby names. We took turns saying various names, none of which either of us liked very much. "Ugh, boys' names are hard," I said after shooting down a few of Chris's suggestions. We sat in silence for a few minutes, brainstorming possible names that would be at least tolerable.

"Ethan Daniel," Chris finally said, his eyes fixed on the road. I thought for a moment. "I like it! Wow, I actually really like it."

Chris smiled, looking ahead. "Me too. Let's add that one to our list." I pulled out my phone and added Ethan Daniel to our digital list of possible names. It was definitely my favorite so far.

We prayed constantly for our boy in the weeks following that first difficult appointment. Each time I prayed,

I almost called him Ethan. I stopped myself each time because we had not named him yet. I shared this with Chris, who said he felt the same way. Ethan was the name we both continually thought of as we referred to our son. We decided to wait to make a final decision. In my mind, I knew he was going to be Ethan.

On the night we returned home from Las Vegas, Chris called our pastor to give him an update and to ask him to pray for us. Our pastor prayed for us and said he would add our request to the church prayer list. "Does he have a name yet?" he asked.

Chris covered the mouthpiece with his hand. "Have we officially named him yet?" he asked me.

I smiled. We both already knew the answer. "Yes, his name is Ethan Daniel Hernandez."

Later, I looked up the meaning of the name Ethan. Ethan is a Hebrew name that means "strong," "safe," and "enduring." I considered these words. I thought back to all of the times I had felt Ethan wiggle and kick in my womb, even before the doctor thought it was too early for me to feel movement. I thought of the somersault he had performed for us in the first ultrasound. He was strong. He was safe. His name would endure.

Someone had told me Ethan is a biblical name. I was not aware of this and I decided to do some research. Ethan is mentioned in 1 Kings 4:31 as a wise man. He was so wise that Solomon was compared to him. "For he [Solomon] was wiser than all other men, wiser than Ethan the Ezrahite." In 1 Chronicles 15:16–17, Ethan is listed as one of the musicians who worshipped God as the Ark of the Covenant was carried to the tent David had prepared.

Ethan was a worshipper. In fact, Ethan wrote Psalm 89. I was fascinated by this discovery and began to copy the entire psalm into my journal.

> *I will sing of the steadfast love of the Lord, forever;*
> *with my mouth I will make known your*
> *faithfulness to all generations.*
> *For I said, "Steadfast love will be built up forever;*
> *in the heavens you will establish your faithfulness."*
> *You have said, "I have made a covenant with my*
> *chosen one;*
> *I have sworn to David my servant:*
> *I will establish your offspring forever,*
> *and build your throne for all generations."*
>
> *(verses 1–4)*

I continued to copy each word into my journal. I really liked where this was going so far. The Lord is faithful and steadfast. He will provide.

> *Let the heavens praise your wonders, O Lord,*
> *your faithfulness in the assembly of the holy ones!*
> *For who in the skies can be compared to the Lord?*
> *Who among the heavenly beings is like the Lord,*
> *a God greatly to be feared in the council of the*
> *holy ones,*
> *and awesome above all who are around him?*
> *O Lord God of hosts,*
> *who is mighty as you are, O Lord,*
> *with your faithfulness all around you?*
> *You rule the raging of the sea;*
> *when its waves rise, you still them.*

You crushed Rahab like a carcass;
you scattered your enemies with your mighty arm.
The heavens are yours; the earth also is yours;
the world and all that is in it, you have founded them.
(verses 5–11)

I felt such comfort reflecting on the might and the sovereignty of God. *Lord, you are so much more powerful than I can even begin to comprehend. You created all things. You can save our baby.*

I continued to write, carefully copying each word into my leather-bound journal. The psalmist Ethan goes on to speak of God's promise to David and to David's offspring. He writes of the faithfulness of God. He will never violate His covenant with David's offspring. He will establish their line forever.

Around verse 38, things began to go downhill. I stopped writing and stared at the page.

But now you have cast off and rejected;
you are full of wrath against your anointed.
You have renounced the covenant with your servant;
you have defiled his crown in the dust.

And then down to verses 45 through 51:

You have cut short the days of his youth;
you have covered him with shame.
How long, O Lord? Will you hide yourself forever?
How long will your wrath burn like fire?
Remember how short my time is!
For what vanity you have created all the
    children of man!

What man can live and never see death?
Who can deliver his soul from the power of Sheol?
Lord, where is your steadfast love of old,
which by your faithfulness you swore to David?
Remember, O Lord, how your servants are mocked,
and how I bear in my heart the insults of all the
many nations,
with which your enemies mock, O Lord,
with which they mock the footsteps of your anointed.

I understood this scripture was not written for me specifically and I do not think we should take scripture out of context. As Christians, many times we find a verse and try to twist it to meet our current situation, without considering the original intent of the writer. Even though I knew my Ethan had not written these words, something about the despair at the end bothered me. The beginning of the psalm had brought me such comfort, but the end seemed to pull a rug out from under my feet. Why would God's chosen people feel so abandoned? It seemed as if God had turned His back on them for a time. They were crying out to Him, just as I had. What hope was there for me if God's chosen people were feeling forsaken?

And then I read verse 52. "Blessed be the Lord forever! Amen and Amen." Praise. Genuine praise following despair. The realization struck me hard. The psalmist cried out to God with words of desperation, yet he worshipped at the end. I considered this and realized I was not worshipping God in my despair. I didn't know how, but I wanted to. It occurred to me my feelings of abandonment did not discredit the fact that God was still powerful. He was still in control. He was still faithful. He still "ruled the raging sea," as the psalmist wrote. I needed to worship Him, no matter how bleak the circumstances.

God is steadfast. He is strong. His love endures forever. We continued to search for glimmers of hope at each of the biweekly visits with our perinatologist. Every two weeks, she would conduct an ultrasound and point out Ethan's heart, brain, stomach, and chin. She would measure his growth and print a roll of photographs for us to take home. We would pray before each appointment that this would be the day doctors were stumped by his miraculous healing, but each appointment only brought more somber news and confirmed Ethan would have an extremely difficult road ahead of him. The severity of Ethan's condition seemed to mount with each visit.

I loved our perinatologist and always felt like she was rooting for us—for Ethan. She gave us hope but was honest regarding Ethan's poor health. She was kind and patient as she responded to our seemingly never-ending list of questions.

At the end of one appointment, our perinatologist told us something I have always held on to. "This looks like a baby who was supposed to miscarry but didn't," she said. I think she said this to assure us we could have done nothing to prevent this and to prepare us for the unthinkable. She wanted us to understand Ethan's health condition may be terminal.

But I clung to the final words: "but didn't." He could have miscarried in those first few weeks following conception, but for some reason he didn't. *He is supposed to be here.*

We continued to pray for additional miracles. *God, please give Ethan the strength to continue to fight. I know you have kept him here for a reason. Please protect him. Like his name, make him strong and keep him safe.*

Four

Only good things

When Chris and I learned of Ethan's health concerns, we immediately decided to share the news with our friends and family. We knew we would need support throughout our pregnancy and after Ethan was born, regardless of the outcome, but mostly we wanted prayer. Chris and I both believed (and still do) God is sovereign and He has the power to heal. We asked our friends and family to join us as we prayed for our son. We called close friends and family to share the news of Ethan's diagnosis and posted regular updates on Facebook after each doctor's appointment. We were humbled by the number of people praying for us. Friends and family asked their churches to pray and soon we had prayer warriors joining us from around the country.

I am so thankful for this prayer support. I truly believe God hears and answers prayers. Although I knew God could heal Ethan, I was not convinced He would heal him in the ways I wanted. I knew God would do what was best for our child and for our family, but I also knew there was a possibility God's "best" would look very different than my desired plans. That scared me.

My perspective began to shift as we continued to pray for our baby. One day at church, someone approached Chris and me after hearing about Ethan's struggling health. "You just have to have faith," he said. "God will heal him!" I remember feeling so put off by this statement. Did feeling uncomfortable with this man's words make me a bad Christian? Was I lacking in faith because I thought God could heal Ethan eternally rather than physically? I felt conflicted because I knew God *could* heal Ethan, but I was not convinced He *would*. I immediately thought of Job and David.

In the Bible, the book of Job tells the story of God's goodness in the midst of loss and despair. Job is described as "blameless and upright, one who feared God and turned away from evil" (Job 1:1). This was someone whom most of us would consider a "good guy," yet God allowed Job to lose everything he had. Job lost his children, his possessions, and even his health. In his grief Job did not curse God, but worshipped him. He praised God in spite of the pain and devastation that had swept through his life. God blessed Job for his faithfulness and eventually provided him with more children, possessions, and health.

Then there is the story of David. David, who is often described as "a man after God's own heart," lost his child. 2 Samuel 12 says David's son became very sick. David fasted and prayed, pleading for God to heal him. On the seventh day, the child died. After his child breathed his last, David washed his face, cleaned himself up, and ate. His servants were shocked at David's behavior and asked why he was no longer fasting and weeping. David responded, "While the child was alive, I fasted and wept, for I said, 'Who knows whether the Lord will be gracious to me, that the child may live?' But now he is dead. Why should I fast? Can I bring him back again? I shall go to him, but he will not return to me." David understood the pain of loss, yet he kept his eyes fixed on God. I would imagine David also knew God could have saved his child, yet he continued to praise Him when physical healing didn't come.

If these men of God experienced grief in their lives, who was I to think I was safe from sorrow? I am no better than Job or David. The Bible makes clear that God loved both Job and David, yet He still allowed them to experience incredible loss. I wrestled with that as I responded to the well-meaning instructions of friends to simply "have enough faith." It occurred to me I could not manipulate God, no matter how many "good things" I did. God was and still is far bigger than what I can comprehend. Up until now, I had wanted God to be my spiritual vending machine. Insert prayer here. Receive an answer in a pretty wrapper.

I felt challenged by this realization. I too had said many times, "You just need to have faith!" But can my faith change the will of God? I'm not that powerful. I needed to have faith in His goodness regardless of my circumstances. Yes, I needed to believe in God's ability to do great works in our lives, but I also needed to submit to His perfect will and rest in His infinite wisdom.

Psalm 34:19 says, "Many are the afflictions of the righteous, but the LORD delivers him out of them all." I realized I was never promised an easy life. God is not interested in making my life on earth as comfortable as possible. Yes, he cares for me and he wants what is best for me, but our purpose goes beyond our time here on earth. The best thing God could give me is more of Himself. I may find happiness in this world, but my life on earth is temporary. The biggest blessings are eternal. I wrestled with this because I wanted to have an easy life. Like Jesus prayed in Matthew 6:9–13, our prayers should ask for God's will to be done.

What is the point of prayer then? I wondered.

I didn't know God's will, but I pleaded every day on Ethan's behalf. We still had hope Ethan could be physically healed and we prayed for this to be God's will.

Our appointment in Los Angeles was scheduled for July 20 and I prayed the doctors would not detect anything wrong with our baby. I prayed for God's will to be done in Ethan's life, but always added a request for Ethan to experience complete healing.

July 20 finally came and we drove to Los Angeles for our referral. I was anxious to learn more about what was wrong with Ethan. My stomach was in knots as we drove to the hospital. I continued to pray the doctors would not find any abnormalities. *Show your glory through this, God. The doctors will be stumped that he is okay and they will see that a miracle took place! Please heal him.*

The facility was much bigger than our original hospital. Office buildings were spread out over multiple city blocks and we stopped at a map to orient ourselves. I already felt overwhelmed and the hustle and bustle of the large campus added to my feelings of anxiety. I was thankful Chris was calm, levelheaded, and able to easily locate our building on the map.

My heart was pounding and my palms were sweaty as we rode the elevator to the third floor. A young nurse checked us in for our appointment and led us to a dimly lit examination room. She welcomed us to have a seat and assured us that both doctors would be with us soon. I looked around the room and wondered why the lights were so dim. I already felt like a gloomy shadow was hanging over me and the ambiance did not help. I nervously fidgeted with my hands and looked over at my husband. He seemed calm and flashed me a reassuring smile. I took a deep breath and tried to relax.

The door opened with a squeak. The Los Angeles perinatologist entered the room and introduced himself to both of us. "I looked at your file and saw your appointment history, but I want to take a second look today to get a closer look at your baby. Hopefully this visit will give you more answers and help us create a plan. Our pediatric cardiologist will join us in a few minutes. For now, go ahead and lay back and we'll get started with the ultrasound." A large screen was erected on the wall in front of me, allowing Chris and me to see everything the doctor was seeing.

The door squeaked again and another man entered, dressed in a white coat. He warmly introduced himself as the pediatric cardiologist. He joined the perinatologist and they both peered at images of our baby on the monitor. They spoke to one another using medical terms I did not understand. There was a look of seriousness on both their faces as they pointed to the screen, took notes, and talked using words that felt like a foreign language to me.

Finally, the doctors seemed to reach some sort of conclusion. One of them reached for a light switch and the room brightened. It felt a little less dreary. *Finally.*

They took turns explaining the results of the ultrasound. I tried to focus on the doctors' words and did my best to comprehend the terms used as they illustrated a picture for us. It was confirmed Ethan was missing a piece of his cerebellum and he had pockets of fluid on his brain. We would not know how these defects would affect his brain function until after he was born. The missing piece, coupled with the fluid, could result in minimal to severe brain damage. His heart defect was even more severe than we had originally thought, with a large atrial septal defect (ASD) and heart vessels that appeared to be jumbled and wrapped around his trachea. The list of concerns continued. One of the doctors explained Ethan had a small chin, which was positioned in such a way that it could block his airway and make it difficult for him to breathe independently. On top of this, his tiny body was measuring a few weeks behind schedule.

"When we see this many concerns, the best conclusion is that the baby has some sort of genetic disorder or chromosomal defect," one of the doctors said.

Chris watched the doctor intently, holding on to every word. "But he could be okay, right? Is there a chance this could be nothing?"

The cardiologist leaned back in his chair and folded his arms, seeming to carefully consider the best response. When he spoke, it was with the gentleness and clarity of a caring teacher. "Imagine you are flying over a busy freeway interchange," he began. "From the sky, you can see there are many cars on the freeway. You may even be able to label some of them. That car is red, that car is green, that car is expensive, that car must be very old," he said, using his index finger to point at the imaginary cars. "But you can see only so much from the sky. If a car looks old, it may be in great condition or it could be in need of a mechanic. In this position, we can make assumptions, but it is impossible to know more until you actually get down on the ground and open the hood of the car.

"An ultrasound is similar. We try to make as many assumptions as we can, but there is a lot we cannot know based on a picture. Oftentimes when there are many obvious concerns, there are more concerns under the surface that we simply have not discovered yet. I have seen enough concerns to make me fear there are more concerns under the surface. We won't really know until we get a closer look. "Of course, there is always the chance that everything could be okay. At this point, we simply do not know. Conducting an amniocentesis test may give you these answers."

We had considered the amniocentesis earlier in the pregnancy, but had declined due to the risks of preterm labor. Again we considered our options, asked questions, and weighed the pros and cons. The test would tell us with certainty whether Ethan had a trisomy disorder or another genetic condition, giving us a better idea of what to expect and how to prepare for a child with unique needs. Once again it was explained to us that the test would only allow us to prepare and would not give the doctors any information that may be valuable in treating Ethan. They would treat him the same regardless of the test results. We decided we were willing to wait for answers. I didn't want to look back and wonder what I could have done differently. We didn't want to risk it.

The doctor nodded as we told him our decision to decline the amniocentesis. "So you are sure you want this baby?" The words sounded more like a statement than a question.

It was not the first time we had been asked this question, but it still felt like a punch in the gut each time. I wanted this precious baby more than anything. I had wanted this for so long. I would have willingly traded places with him if it were possible.

We discussed our plan moving forward. The perinatologist wanted me to deliver in Los Angeles so we could have access to specialized care. If everything went according to plan, I would have a scheduled EXIT cesarean delivery. The perinatologist explained the medical team would begin a classic cesarean, but would only deliver Ethan's head and shoulders at first. A doctor would work on Ethan to establish an airway before he was disconnected from the placenta so he could continue to get oxygen through the umbilical cord.

"Do you have some time?" the perinatologist asked. "Would you be interested in taking a tour of the hospital? I'd love to spend more time discussing your birth plan, but I have an appointment with another patient in a few minutes. If you have the time, we can meet after the tour." Chris and I agreed it would be nice to discuss our birth plan in further detail and to receive a tour of the hospital. We made arrangements to meet back in about an hour.

We stepped outside into the warm July afternoon and walked across the street toward the main hospital. The sidewalk bustled with pedestrian traffic. I wondered where each person was headed. How many of them had sick children in the hospital? How many of them were sick themselves? How many of these people were doing everything they could to simply hold it together?

I soaked in the sights of the busy street lined with medical buildings on both sides. I was suddenly struck by the harsh realization we were not the only family with a sick child. Here stood buildings filled with children walking through incredible suffering. I could not imagine how many were in the city of Los Angeles alone. It hurt my heart to think of how many sick babies there must be in the entire world. I struggled to stand under the crushing reality of just how broken the world is.

I cried as we walked back to the perinatologist's office, not just for me, but for every family around the world that has had to watch their child fight for their life. I hit a low point after our appointment in Los Angeles. I had been holding on to a hope that Ethan would be miraculously healed. I could picture the confusion on the doctors' faces as they peered at the ultrasound, unable to find any abnormalities. We would laugh with tears pouring down our faces and praise God for His goodness. Instead, we left each appointment feeling more discouraged than we had felt when we walked in.

I struggled to be around other people. It felt incredibly vulnerable to update well-meaning people on the latest appointment and to watch their hopeful smiles turn into an empathic frown. But somehow it was even worse when they continued to smile in response to another somber appointment. I felt like I might lose my mind if one more person told me to "keep my chin up" or "just have faith." It felt easiest to withdraw and hide. I felt defeated, forgotten, and so very disappointed. I longed for closeness with God, but church was the last place I wanted to be.

I tried for a while. I continued to sing on the worship team and Chris and I continued to teach Sunday school, until one week it suddenly felt like too much. I broke down sobbing in the parking lot and couldn't bring myself to get out of the car. I felt like the biggest hypocrite. How was I supposed to teach children about God's love when I didn't feel loved by Him? Chris wiped my tears as I vented my frustrations and lovingly excused me to leave. "Take the car," he said gently. "I can teach Sunday School for us." I hated to bail on him, but he insisted it would be okay and I welcomed the opportunity to escape.

I felt refreshed as I drove back to church to give Chris a ride home. I slipped inside and ran straight into our pastor's wife, Debbie. Her eyes were filled with genuine care and I knew she was familiar with this grief, possibly even better than I was standing in the middle of it. She and our pastor had lost their son Adrian to a fatal birth defect thirty years prior. She had reached out to me throughout the difficult weeks that followed Ethan's diagnosis. She shared tears with me and was a safe place for me to share my innermost feelings. My worst fear had been a reality for her.

She pulled me into a motherly hug and I immediately felt the invitation to be vulnerable. "How are you doing?" she asked.

"I couldn't be here today," I admitted as tears filled my eyes. "I just couldn't face anyone. I am tired of people telling me how to feel. I am tired of feeling so tired. I know God is in control, but I can't understand why He would allow this to happen. I'm so angry at Him."

Debbie didn't scold me for my anger, but rather she welcomed my honesty. "It's okay to tell Him that," she said gently. "It's okay to feel all of those things. You are human and this hurts.

"People will try to comfort you and, yes, they will say things that feel unnecessary. They care, but they are only human too.

"But when you feel angry, you can turn to God with that anger. Talk to Him. Fight with Him. Bring your fears to Him and seek answers. He can take it."

I welcomed the hot tears that streaked down my face. I felt welcomed and understood.

We talked for a few more minutes before Debbie said something I'll never forget. She gently took my hand in hers and tears filled her own eyes. "No matter what happens,

God will not leave you empty-handed. You may not receive what you asked for, but He will only give you good things."

Only good things. Somber waiting rooms, life-threatening birth defects, and sleepless nights felt anything but good, yet I clung to this promise. I searched my Bible as I wrestled with anger, confusion, and doubt. I brought my anger to God, often with tears and a raised voice. *Have You forgotten me? Do You care? Are You good?*

In Matthew 7:11, Jesus says, "If you then, who are evil, know how to give good gifts to your children, how much more will your Father who is in heaven give good things to those who ask him!" God provides for us like a caring father provides for His children. Not just any father, but a perfect Father. In my wrestling, I asked God to remind me of this truth. I asked Him to help me trust Him when I doubted His goodness. I asked Him to give me eyes to see what is truly "good."

As I continued to search, I came across Romans 8:28. In this verse Paul says, "And we know that for those who love God all things work together for good, for those who are called according to his purpose." God works all things together for good. Not just some things. All things for those who are called according to his purpose. I had read this passage countless times before, but it wasn't until that moment I realized Paul never said all the bad things that happen to us are actually good things. He never said sin, evil, and death are good. Sometimes "bad" things enter our lives. Prisoners being tortured for their beliefs. Sexual abuse. An orphan dying of starvation. Injustice against the helpless. There is no denying the brokenness and evil within these scenarios—scenarios that break God's heart. Yet nothing is beyond Christ's redemption. He works all things, even the most unimaginable heartaches, into good for His children. As the ultimate enemy of death, God sent Jesus to conquer death and to rescue us from our sin. Jesus came to provide hope to the hopeless. He came to give us an opportunity to spend eternity in paradise with Christ. He came to give life. He will come back again to make all things right and to destroy evil for eternity. He will work all things together for our good.

I began to wonder if my definition of "good" lined up with God's definition of good. I wondered if my plans might look different than His purpose. It is so easy for me to think of the "good" things on this earth–temporary things I can reach out and feel, like food, clothing, health, financial security, good coffee, and chocolate cheesecake. All of these things are good and worth thanking God for, yet none of these things will remain forever. God works all things, even broken things, together for the good of His children. Not for a shallow "good" that will fade away, but for an eternal good. It challenges me to think of how my heart often longs for those temporary things, rather than the eternal things that will truly satisfy me.

I thought of this a few days later when Chris came home with a beaming smile and news to share. "My whole office gathered to pray today," he said. "It was amazing!" He told me how a few of his coworkers had heard about Ethan and invited the entire office to meet in the conference room at the end of the day to pray. Everyone showed up.

"A few of my coworkers told me they have not prayed in a long time, but walking through this with us made them want to be closer to God," he said excitedly. "A lot of people have been asking me questions about our faith. This situation with Ethan has created such an opportunity to share Jesus with them and to explain the hope we can have in Christ!

"And do you know what I realized? We've been praying for months that God would use Ethan in big ways. Even before you got pregnant we prayed He would use our child. Today I realized God is already answering that prayer in ways I would never have imagined."

I smiled and voiced my excitement, but deep down I felt resistant. My flesh waged within me and I selfishly didn't want God to answer our prayer in this way. I wanted Him to use Ethan's life and his words to impact the world. I didn't want Him to use Ethan's suffering to have an impact on the world. *Please don't let this be the end of the story, God. Please save our baby.*

Debbie's words came into my mind once again. *God will not leave you empty-handed.*

I knew God was already answering our prayer in ways I never could have imagined or planned myself. He had heard us. He knew what was best. Ethan had a purpose I did not know yet. I took a deep breath. *Help me to trust you, God.*

A few weeks before Ethan was born, I put words to my worst fear for the first time. I was catching up with one of my oldest and dearest friends when she asked me how she could be praying for our family. "What are you struggling with the most right now?" she asked compassionately. I hadn't said it out loud until that moment. Of course I knew things could turn out this way, but I had pushed the idea into the back of my mind and tried to think positively. Somehow I felt suppressing my fears would make them less likely to unfold. Saying it out loud was terrifying, yet I welcomed the opportunity to be honest about my biggest worry.

"I'm afraid Ethan will die," I said. "My biggest fear is he'll die young, before he ever has the chance to experience life and before I ever have the chance to experience motherhood."

It may sound strange, but I had a realization as soon as I spoke the words. Call it intuition, call it the Holy Spirit, but the message felt so clear to me. *My biggest fear would be Ethan's greatest joy.* For God's children, death means eternal healing from any sickness or complications. Death for Ethan would mean he would never experience pain or fear. He would forever be in the presence of Jesus. Still, even believing this with all my heart, I desperately wanted him to be with me.

My weary heart began to ponder the fragility of life and the sovereignty of God. None of us is guaranteed tomorrow. We are all mortal. Death is inevitable and life is a vapor. In the incomprehensible span of eternity, our lives are just a dot. What would I do with that tiny dot? How could I celebrate Ethan's life, no matter how long or how short?

As challenging as the last few weeks of my pregnancy were, those days were also some of the sweetest. Chris and I set out to celebrate Ethan's life however we could. We prayed he would feel safe and loved even in my womb. I sang songs to Ethan while I cooked dinner and Chris read him stories. We told him about our day and pointed out things we saw. We prayed for him every night and told him we loved him before we fell asleep at the end of another tiring day.

We prepared his nursery. We laughed, cried, and laughed some more as Chris painted the walls and assembled his crib. I had always wanted to have a woodland nursery theme for our first baby, complete with baby foxes, deer, and bear cubs. Before long, Ethan's room had been transformed into an adorable forest.

We continued to check in with my perinatologist every other week. She and the Los Angeles team had worked out an arrangement for me to continue care with her before delivering in L.A. I was thankful for the opportunity to continue to see her. I always felt cared for by her and could trust her to be honest yet compassionate.

"He's still measuring small, but he's growing at a consistent rate," she said to me as she wiped the warm gel off my stomach. We had just completed another routine ultrasound and received a roll of adorable 3-D photos to take home. "The spacing in his brain has remained stable and I'm pleased it is not spreading. As you get closer to thirty weeks, you'll start to have more regular appointments with the hospital in L.A. since that is where you will be delivering. They will probably give you a date for your scheduled cesarean as it gets closer."

"What happens if I go into labor?" I asked.

"I recommend you come here so we can take care of you, instead of driving to L.A.," she said. "I would hate for you to get stuck in traffic and find yourself in an emergency situation on the side of the freeway. If you come here, there is a good chance we would be able to slow down your labor and transport you to L.A. Call us ahead of time so we can be ready for you. I may not be the one delivering your baby, but the doctor on call will be able to review your file and prepare for you. Do you have the number for Labor and Delivery?"

I nodded.

"You never know with babies," she added. "They come when they want."

We left her office feeling hopeful. Ethan was growing and his heartbeat was strong. He could be okay. We knew God was sovereign and He cared about our family. We continued to pray for complete healing over our baby. We were confident He could do it. He would not leave us empty-handed.

Five

August 16

I woke up on the morning of August 15 feeling as if I had run a marathon. I'm one of those early risers who usually jumps out of bed without hitting the snooze button, but on this particular day I could barely muster the strength to roll out of bed. My petite frame was growing larger and larger each day and I chalked it up to typical third-trimester exhaustion. I forced myself to take a shower before collapsing back into bed, my wet hair still wrapped up in a towel. My back hurt and my stomach felt unsettled. I had a to-do list a mile long and this was the last way I wanted to spend my Saturday. *You can do this,* I told myself as I tried to shake off the tiredness and stay on task.

Chris encouraged me to rest, but I was determined to push through and went to the grocery store. Walking around the store gave me the burst of energy I needed. Chris and I ran more errands together throughout the afternoon, including stopping by a hardware store to make a copy of our house key. We had recently realized no one else had a key to our house, which could become a problem if I unexpectedly went into labor without my hospital bag or while our dog was locked inside. We later placed the key on our kitchen counter with the intention of giving it to my parents the next time we saw them. That detail is pretty ironic, but I'll come back to that later.

We savored a quiet Saturday afternoon at home together. We watched a goofy Adam Sandler movie and made miniature pizzas on English muffins. Chris massaged my aching back and we enjoyed a quiet date night at home.

I noticed a very small streak of light pink blood in my underwear before I went to bed that night. My heart raced and my stomach dropped. I told Chris what I had seen and we called the advice nurse immediately. The nurse cautioned me to watch for any changes, but reassured me it was likely harmless if the bleeding was light and if I was not experiencing contractions. She encouraged me to go to the hospital if I experienced any changes during the night or if my intuition told me something was wrong. "Call us when you're on your way and we'll be ready for you," she said.

We considered our options. Our hospital was forty-five minutes away from our house and it would be a quick trip to check on things. I thought back to the two times we had rushed to the hospital in a panic over first-trimester spotting and nothing had been wrong. My back had been sore for days, but I wasn't in any other pain. We decided to wait it out and drive over to the hospital if things got worse or if I was still spotting in the morning. I was completely exhausted and sleep felt like an easy choice.

Have you ever woken up from a deep sleep because you felt like you were falling? Your eyes shoot open and you desperately scramble for something to hold on to before realizing you are safe in your own bed. That's the best way I can describe what it felt like to wake up later that night, except I was met with dread instead of relief when I recognized my surroundings.

My eyes shot open and it took a moment for me to orient myself. *Where am I? What time is it? What is that sensation I'm feeling?*

I had always wondered what it would feel like for my water to break and now I knew. "No, no, no!" the words leapt from my mouth involuntarily as fluid rushed out of me.

Chris quickly rolled over in bed to face me. "What's wrong?"

"My water is breaking," I said, reaching for the light on the nightstand. I glanced at the clock and saw that it was only 11:30. I quickly hurried to the bathroom as water continued to gush out of me. I had no idea my body could hold so much fluid.

My heart pounded in my chest. I knew there is no turning back once your water is broken. "This is happening. This is real," I said to Chris. I felt slightly panicked and my mind flashed back through the past few months. *Will he survive? I'm far enough along that it's likely. What about his health? He has so many health issues. Oh Jesus, please protect him.*

Chris quickly began to gather our belongings as I sat over the toilet, amniotic fluid continuing to pour out. We knew we needed to follow Plan B. At this point, a planned C-section in Los Angeles seemed out of the question. We needed to get to our original hospital. This hospital was about forty-five minutes away from our house, but it definitely beat the ninety-minute drive to Los Angeles.

I called Labor and Delivery to let them know we were on our way. The typically busy freeway was nearly empty as we sped toward the hospital. I thanked God for His grace in allowing us to go into labor near midnight on a weekend, rather than during rush hour on a weekday.

We arrived on the Labor and Delivery floor and a nurse asked Chris to sit in the waiting room while I was assessed in triage. The on-call doctor, a kind woman with dark-rimmed glasses and a reassuring smile, explained our next steps, including checking my cervix to see how my labor was progressing and to determine my water had truly broken. She also wanted to check Ethan.

"Let's take a look at him," she said, squeezing warm gel onto my belly. "I just want to make sure he's doing okay." She stared at the screen for a few moments and did not say anything. The brief silence made me worry.

"Are you in any pain right now?" she asked me, peering intently at the screen.

I shook my head. "Not really. My back is a bit achy, but it's been like that all week."

"I ask because you're having a really big contraction right now." She pointed out my tightened abdomen. "Do you see what your tummy is doing?"

My jaw dropped. This was nothing like I had expected labor to feel and I could hardly believe what I was seeing. "I've felt some tightening throughout the week, but I'm not in any pain," I told her.

"You must have a very high pain tolerance, honey! I can't even get a good look at your baby right now because the contraction is so strong. We'll wait for it to pass and then we'll take a look." We waited for the contraction to pass before she took a look at Ethan and detected a strong, healthy heartbeat.

Next she checked my cervix. "You're three centimeters dilated and there's no turning back at this point. You're definitely not leaving this hospital until you deliver. Our hope is to delay delivery for at least forty-eight hours so there is time to administer two doses of a steroid shot to prepare your baby's premature lungs to breathe outside the womb. In the meantime, we'll get you settled into a room and will give you some magnesium in hopes of slowing down your labor so the steroids have more time to reach your baby."

A nurse gave me the first dose of the steroid shots, inserted my IV line, and moved me into a comfortable room on the Labor and Delivery wing, where Chris was able to join me. I was surprised at how nice the rooms were. Each one looked like a hotel room, complete with a comfortably sized hospital bed, a window seat that pulled out into a twin bed, a dresser, a television, and a private bathroom.

We checked into our room and my parents arrived to retrieve our house keys so they could take our dog to their house (remember that extra set of keys that never made it off our kitchen counter? Thanks, Mom and Dad, for coming to get our keys and rescue our dog in the middle of the night).

By now it was past 2:00 a.m. and we were encouraged to get some rest. A doctor would stop by in the morning to discuss a plan for Ethan's delivery. They would also consult with my doctor in Los Angeles to determine if I should be transported to that hospital for the planned procedure.

I tried to sleep, but it seemed nearly impossible with an IV in one arm, a blood pressure cuff on the other, one monitor on my abdomen to check my contractions, and another to monitor Ethan's heart rate. Alarms sounded when Ethan wiggled away from the monitor and each time my IV ran out. A nurse entered the room to check my vitals each hour and the blood pressure cuff constricted my arm every thirty minutes. I rested my eyes, listening to the beating of

Ethan's heart on the monitor. His heart rate was strong and it brought me such comfort to hear. Every now and then he'd get the hiccups and the monitor would pick up the sweet sound. Neither Chris nor I got much sleep and I felt relieved when sunlight began to peek through the window. I ordered breakfast and met our day shift nurse, whom we'll call Anne. Each hour, Anne came in to check my vitals and would ask me to describe my pain level on a scale of one to ten. I'd give her a report of how many contractions I had felt in the past hour and she would check my contraction monitor to confirm my count. Sometimes I wasn't really sure if I had had a contraction and I would ask her to check my monitor to see. I could tell my uterus was tight at various times, but I still hadn't felt much pain, other than menstrual-like cramps and an aching back.

Chris sat close by my side the entire time. Throughout the long night and into the morning, Chris never left me. At one point, I encouraged him to leave so he could eat something. Sleeping on the couch all night was not comfortable and I knew he had not gotten much sleep. I had shared some breakfast with him, but it wasn't much. I assured him my contractions had calmed down, but he refused to leave. I finally talked him into grabbing a snack at a nearby vending machine. As much as I wanted him to take care of himself, it was incredibly comforting to have him close by.

My stomach felt sick with nerves as we waited to hear from the doctor. Dressed in a scratchy hospital gown, sitting on a bed still damp from my broken water, and anxious over our unborn child, I knew the only thing that could truly bring me peace in that moment. I reached for my phone so I could read the Bible from an app. I had been reading through Psalms over the past few weeks and that morning's daily reading was from Psalm 116.

The writer (likely David) begins the passage by declaring love for the Lord. With awe, he proclaims how the Lord preserved his life and showed him mercy. He speaks of the ways God delivers us and protects us. He vows to serve the Lord with his life. Peace washed over me as I continued to read.

Then the words of verse 15 jumped off the page at me. "Precious in the sight of the LORD is the death of his saints." Oof. Feelings of dread and comfort waged within me. On one hand, these words felt like a punch in the gut. The death of God's children is precious to Him? On the other hand, I felt secure pondering the way God views our souls as precious. I thought about what death means for the believer—eternity with Christ—and about the mercy God shows us. I wrestled through both comfort and frustration. Was God trying to prepare my heart for something I did not want to face? Honestly, I hoped not. I prayed these words were simply a coincidence and not a divine reminder of God's care for us in death. I did not want to say goodbye to Ethan, no matter how precious his soul was to God. I pleaded that God would not take our baby too soon. It is a bit painful to confess that I didn't want to accept the way God, in His great compassion and goodness, was speaking to me from His Word and mercifully preparing me for what was to come.

It wasn't that long until I felt a contraction that was a bit stronger than the others. I've had painful menstrual cramps since I was a teenager and describe it as comparable to the worst cramps I've felt. Still, I always expected labor to be incredibly worse than what I was experiencing.

It was probably nothing to worry about, but I decided to let my nurse know.

"Anne, I just had another contraction and that one was a little worse than the others. I think they're getting stronger," I told her.

"It's possible your contractions are getting stronger because you aren't emptying your bladder all the way. A full bladder can cause your contractions to speed up. I think it may be time to get a catheter," she suggested.

Ugh. I had been doing everything I could to avoid the catheter. I was attached to my bed, thanks to the IV and monitors, which meant my only options were a bedpan or a catheter. I gladly opted for the bedpan as it seemed desirable compared to the catheter. I had hoped to avoid it altogether, but agreed it was time.

Just as Anne was preparing to insert the catheter, two doctors entered my room: one from the NICU and one from Labor and Delivery. They introduced themselves before explaining that, though this hospital had an outstanding NICU, the hospital in Los Angeles may be better equipped for Ethan's particular needs. They had already consulted with the medical team in L.A. and the decision was made to transfer me into their care.

"I'm going to do a quick exam to make sure your labor is not progressing too quickly and make sure you are stable enough to be transported to Los Angeles," the on-call obstetrician said. "How have your contractions been?"

"They haven't been too painful," I said.

"I was just about to insert a catheter," Anne added. The obstetrician asked Anne to insert the catheter while she continued to review the plans for our transfer and delivery in L.A.

Excruciating pain immediately radiated through my body as the catheter was inserted. My entire body recoiled under the worst pain I had ever felt in my life. I began to shake uncontrollably and my teeth began to chatter. The sensation took me by surprise, as I had felt fairly comfortable just moments prior.

I tried to form words to describe what I was feeling, but a low moan escaped instead. I felt breathless. "It hurts," I managed to squeak.

"The catheter may burn for a moment," Anne said. "But you should feel more comfortable in a few seconds." The pain did not ease up. If anything, it was growing more intense by the second.

"Yeah, no. It's getting worse," I said, my teeth still chattering.

The obstetrician looked concerned and asked me to describe the pain. I tried to catch my breath and formulate clear words. "Ow. Yeah, it feels like burning. And pressure. Like I have to pee but I can't. Oh man, this hurts." Chills continued to shake my body.

"I'd like to check your cervix," the obstetrician said, as she crouched down to examine me. A moment later, she stood up and gently took my hand in hers. "Honey, you're eight centimeters dilated and I can touch your baby's bottom. You're in transition and we aren't going to transport you anywhere. You're going to have this baby right now."

"We need to get her into an emergency C-section." The words had barely left her lips when a swarm of medical personnel descended on our room. It seemed as if the room was spinning. Like we were living in a dream. Everything happened so quickly. Someone handed Chris a pair of medical scrubs to change into and instructed him to wait in another area just outside the operating room. Meanwhile, my entire bed was wheeled down the hall toward the operating room, leaving my husband behind. I tried to breathe and distract myself from the pain. I felt terrified. So many "what-ifs" would finally be answered and I was not sure if I was ready for the final answers.

Once I was in the operating room Anne told me they needed to move me from my bed to the operating table. I was in so much pain I could hardly move. My whole body was still shaking. I couldn't tell if I was shaking from pain, from fear, or a combination of both.

Anne placed her hands on my shoulders and began to coach me. "You're doing so good, honey," she said in a motherly way. "You got this far all by yourself. Keep breathing." She continued to coach me as a large needle was inserted into my back, sending the medicine through my body that quickly made my lower half go numb and the pain fade away. She helped me move from my bed and onto the operating table.

The room buzzed with activity. I cannot remember all of the people in the operating room, but I'd imagine there were at least eight between the doctors, nurses, and anesthesiologists assigned to Ethan and me.

My body was still trembling, likely from a combination of fear, adrenaline, and hormones, and I just wanted Chris with me. The door to the operating room swung open each time staff entered the room and each time I hoped it was him. I knew he could not be with me until the local anesthesia fully kicked in and I hoped it would be quick.

I laid on the operating table, staring up at the bright light above me. A doctor placed a curtain in front of me so I could not see anything below my chest. The pain slowly started to ease, as my legs and abdomen gradually went numb.

Chris finally entered the room dressed in medical scrubs and was allowed to sit beside me. I was so happy to see him. He held my hand and I could tell the top half of my body was still trembling.

"I'm really scared," I said to Chris. "Can we pray?" Chris squeezed my hand and prayed. We prayed for peace. We prayed for the doctors. We prayed for Ethan. My anxiety began to wane. By the time Chris said "Amen," a nurse rushed away carrying a baby to the incubator across the room.

"Is that our baby?" Chris asked, shocked at how quickly he had been born. Of course we both knew it was Ethan, but we were in awe at how fast the emergency cesarean had been performed.

"One thirty-two p.m.," someone said. "It's a girl!" Chris and I both looked at each other, our eyes wide in shock.

"Oops. Never mind, it's a boy!"

In the middle of the chaos and fear, we welcomed the opportunity to release some pressure and giggle over the mix-up. Ethan had been keeping us on our toes from day one, and it came as no surprise he'd try to trick us by hiding his male anatomy at birth. Worn from months of unknowns and a sleepless night of waiting, we laughed.

After months of prayerful waiting, Ethan Daniel Hernandez was finally here.

Six

Ninety-three minutes

I had dreamed about this moment for years. What would it feel like to push our first child into the world and hear their cry? Would I weep tears of intense joy, relief, and love when they were finally laid on my chest and I looked into their eyes for the first time? Would the sweetness of the moment cause me to instantly forget about the pain of childbirth, as so many women had told me before?

This was nothing like the scene I had envisioned. Instead of an infant's cries, there were beeps and verbal directives from doctors. Instead of relief, there was fear. The pain didn't dissipate when our baby was born; it only seemed to creep deeper into my heart.

Ethan was laid on an incubator, where an entire medical team surrounded him. I craned my neck to try to catch a glimpse of our boy, but I couldn't see over their shoulders. "What's he doing?" I asked desperately. "Is he breathing? Is he moving?"

Chris stood from the chair beside my head and walked toward the commotion. Amidst the beeping, whirring, and hurried voices, I heard numbers being called out. The numbers were fairly high at first, but started to fall. I tried to make sense of the sounds and shouted numbers. It took me a moment to recognize these numbers were Ethan's heart rate and oxygen saturation levels. They were dropping fast. "Come on up here, Dad," one of the doctors said, inviting Chris to squeeze into the huddle and see our baby boy. Chris entered the tight circle and saw sweet Ethan for the first time. Chris gripped Ethan's tiny hand as the doctors performed compressions on his tiny chest to keep his failing heart beating.

This is where it gets really hard. It's hard to write. It's hard to relive these moments. It's hard to read. I cannot accurately describe the hope, the fear, the worry, and the helplessness I felt at that moment, as I lay numb on the operating table with my body splayed open. I was stitched back together to the soundtrack of the doctors calling out dropping numbers. I heard Chris calling out to Ethan over the beeps and buzzes, rooting for our son to pull through. It brings fresh tears to my eyes just to think of it.

"Come on, Ethan! You can do it, baby," Chris cheered him on, with desperation in his voice. "Come on, Ethan. Come on, baby!"

The doctors continued to perform compressions on Ethan's tiny chest.

Time passed. The numbers continued to get lower.

"Sixty!"

"Forty-five!"

"Come on, baby! I'm right here, Ethan!"

His stats were dropping.

I started crying. Praying. Desperately trying to do anything I could from my helpless position on the operating table.

A doctor approached me. "I'm sorry, Mrs. Hernandez. We did everything we could," she said, with no emotion in her voice. "We need to stop trying to resuscitate him." She seemed distant and guarded, as if she had delivered those heartbreaking words a million times in her career.

Hot tears poured from my eyes like a waterfall. *Everything? Did they really do everything? What happened? His heart rate was so strong when he was first born! I had laid awake listening to his heartbeat the night before! I had felt him kick an hour ago! He was so strong!*

Chris was quickly by my side. He followed the doctor as she walked away. I didn't hear their conversation at the time, but he filled me in later.

"Are you sure there is absolutely nothing else you can do for him?" Chris asked, desperately searching for any option possible.

The doctor explained Ethan's body was simply too broken. He was not circulating blood correctly throughout his body. His tiny airway was blocked and doctors had been unable to intubate him. Even under the best circumstances, intubation would have failed because of his circulation issue, heart defect, and failing organs.

Our tiny baby still had life in him, but his numbers continued to fall. The room grew quieter. We were asked if we wanted to hold him. Of course we wanted nothing more.

Ethan's tiny body was wrapped in a soft white receiving blanket, with red, yellow, and green bunnies on it. A blue and pink striped beanie was placed on his head. It was much too big for his premature frame, but he looked so cute in what seemed like a giant hat.

A doctor gently placed Ethan into Chris's arms. Chris sat by my head and lowered our son close to my face so I could see him. I gazed at his face and suddenly understood what I had been told my entire life; you fall madly in love with your child the moment you first see them. Despite how tiny he was, he had the perfect proportions of a full-term baby—he was simply smaller. At that moment, I never wanted anything more. I would've gladly died in his place, again and again. Meeting Ethan was the most joyous yet most devastating experience of my life.

Chris stood up from his crouched position with Ethan nestled snugly in his arms. The next moments will be engraved in my mind forever. I watched as Chris kissed Ethan's face, walked to the corner of the room, knelt to the ground and cried tears of intense love and deep sorrow. I had seen Chris cry only twice in the seven years I had known him, and I had never seen him weep so openly.

Once the doctors were done stitching me up, I was able to hold Ethan for the first time. I nuzzled my face to his and savored his newborn smell. I snuggled his warm body against me and tried to memorize the way he felt against my chest. I stared at his face, tears pouring from my eyes, and tried to memorize every detail. His adorable baby nose. His kissable little lips. His baby-soft skin. The dark hair on his head. He had Chris's thick hair, just as I had always hoped.

Ethan was bigger than we had expected him to be. When I had met with my doctor earlier that week, she had predicted that Ethan weighed about one and a half pounds. He was a whopping two pounds two ounces and fourteen and three-quarter inches long. He was twelve weeks premature and surprised all of us with his size and the baby fat that had already started to fill out his little body.

Several nurses lifted me from the operating table and onto a hospital bed before wheeling me over to a recovery area. The recovery area was a long room with spaces for multiple beds, with curtains between each bed for privacy.

It was intended for medical staff to monitor patients in the hour after a C-section.

Over the next hour, Chris and I took every moment to cuddle our precious baby. We sang to him, we prayed over him, we kissed his sweet face, and we took photos of him. We knew our time was short and we tried to capture every memory we possibly could. Anne asked me if I wanted to have skin-to-skin contact with him. Of course I did. She unbundled him and laid him against my chest. We savored every minute.

At 3:05 p.m., a doctor came in to check Ethan's heart. He had been lifeless since he had first been laid in my arms and the doctor confirmed what I already knew. His heart had completely stopped beating. Official time of death: 3:05 p.m.

We had known for weeks there was a chance Ethan could die, but it did not make the pain any easier to bear. Even after the doctors had told us there was nothing they could do, we had clung to hope. *Maybe he just needs us. Maybe he'll gain strength after spending time in our arms. It'll be a miracle...*

The official proclamation of his death felt surreal. In the back of my mind I kept thinking, *Maybe they are wrong. Maybe he's just sleeping. Maybe he'll come back. Maybe...*

He didn't come back. Ethan was more alive than ever, rejoicing with Christ. His broken body had been healed for all of eternity. Though I took comfort in this, the pain of being left behind in this cruel world felt unbearable. We were not mourning Ethan's future. We were mourning *our* future on earth. A life without our baby boy. For the first time in my life, I yearned for heaven.

We stared at his face and he looked so peaceful. I am so thankful he did not suffer. It appeared he had simply fallen asleep, drifting into the arms of our Savior. At that moment, I missed him as if he had been gone a hundred years. I longed for him to come back to us.

"You don't have a heart defect any more, baby," I whispered to him as I gently stroked his soft cheeks and kissed his forehead. "You're perfect. You'll never have to have open-heart surgery. You'll never struggle for breath. You're completely healed, Ethan." Tears poured from my eyes. God had healed him. Completely. Although I knew my words were true, I longed for him to come back to us.

Anne had been close by the entire time so she could monitor my recovery, but also gave us our space as a family. "You can have as much time as you need to say goodbye," she said. "Take your time. There is no hurry.

"I also want you to know the doctors worked very hard to save him. I see a lot of births. Usually, doctors will only work on a baby for about fifteen minutes. If the baby's health does not improve and the outcome looks bleak, they usually stop trying after that time. The doctors worked on Ethan for thirty-five minutes. They really wanted to save him. They did everything they could."

Even though we were heartbroken, it meant a lot to know the doctors also had hope for our baby and worked tirelessly to help him.

"I also want you to know something," she said, resting her hand on mine. "I do not think that making it to L.A. would've changed the outcome. It really seems like this was something that could not have been avoided. You both did everything you could to fight for him. Your team did everything they could to fight for him. I don't want you to look back and wonder what could have been done differently. I truly believe you did everything in your power to save him."

I had already begun to wonder what we could have done differently. *What if I had gone to the doctor when I first started feeling uncomfortable last week? What if we had driven to Los Angeles? What if they had done the originally planned EXIT cesarean with my complete medical team on site?* I'm glad Anne shared this reassurance. She seemed very genuine and I believed her, despite only knowing her for a few hours.

It was almost time for me to be moved to my new room where we would be staying for the remainder of our time at the hospital. Our nurse assured us we could have as much time to say goodbye as we needed. We could even keep Ethan's body with us when we moved to a new unit. Chris and I decided it would be best to say goodbye before we moved to our room. We did not want to rush our goodbye to our baby, but we did not want to delay the inevitable either. I never wanted to say goodbye to Ethan. I never wanted to give him up or let anyone else hold him. I wanted to keep him forever. Yet I realized the body I clung to was just a shell. The real Ethan was present with Jesus. The real Ethan was rejoicing. The real Ethan was not here. Even though I knew this, I still felt attached to his body. His small yet perfect body.

We spent another hour holding our sweet baby. We cried millions of tears over him and planted millions of kisses on his face. We cuddled him close and soaked up every memory we possibly could. Then the hardest moment came. We called a nurse and told her we were ready to say goodbye. I gave my firstborn child one last kiss and handed him to the nurse. Sobs shook my body as I watched her carry him out of sight.

Anne returned to our side and told us it was time to move to my new room. I would have to stay in the hospital for another two or three days to recover from surgery.

"Typically, we would take you to a room in Labor and Delivery. There is an area in the hospital where parents stay with their babies. I'd imagine it might be hard to stay in this area for the next few days. Would you like to be moved to a different wing?" she asked.

We were so thankful the staff was considerate and sensitive. "If that's an option, yes please." Arrangements were made to have us moved onto a different wing of the hospital for the remainder of our stay.

Anne wheeled my hospital bed out of the Labor and Delivery wing while Chris walked closely by my side. Hot tears continued to fall from my face. *Goodbye, Ethan.*

There was a button on the wall at the end of the hallway that played a lullaby when it was pushed. It is a tradition for parents to push this button to announce the birth of their child as they are moved from delivery to the postpartum unit. Anne slowed her walk as we approached the button. "Would you like to push it?" she asked.

Chris and I looked at each other and both nodded. "He was here. He was alive. Let's do it. Let's celebrate him." We pushed the button and the lullaby rang through the halls. I broke down crying again as the double doors opened and we departed Labor and Delivery.

We settled into my new room in a different wing of the hospital. Everything felt so surreal. Shortly after moving to my new room, I started to feel queasy. A new nurse was asking me routine questions when I was suddenly struck by an intense wave of nausea. "I'm going to be sick," I said. "Right now." She quickly handed me a bucket as I lost my breakfast. The incision on my abdomen hurt with every heave of my body. As miserable as it felt, it didn't come close to the throbbing ache in my heart.

One of the nurses from Labor and Delivery came by with a beautiful memory box. The soft lavender box was tied together with a silky ribbon and the top unfolded open to reveal its precious contents. The box held the photos the nurse had taken of Ethan, a lock of his thick, black hair, his footprints inked on a piece of paper, a tape measure to record his length, a receiving blanket, and the striped beanie he had been wearing. I wept when I pulled the beanie out of the box. I held it up to my face and inhaled its scent. It still smelled just like him.

The rest of our hospital stay is a blur, but a few details remain clear. Anne came to check on me and say goodbye when her shift ended. I could tell she was crying but trying to conceal it as she walked away. A few family members came to visit with us. A food service worker asked "Where is the baby?" when dropping off dinner. I answered with as much poise as I could muster and, judging by the horrified look on his face, he'll never ask that question to a postpartum patient without a baby in their room again.

I was discharged on Tuesday morning, nearly forty-eight hours after Ethan's birth. You'd think I'd be ready to leave the hospital gown, constant beeping, and traumatic memories behind me, but I felt connected to this place. A whole lifetime had been lived within the walls of the hospital. Those on my medical team are the only people besides Chris and myself who knew Ethan while he was still alive. The best and worst moments of my life were shoved into a three-day span and a piece of my life would always be on the third floor.

Leaving the hospital was the second hardest part of the entire experience. An assistant brought a wheelchair to my room and wheeled me through the halls, through the lobby, and out into the parking lot while Chris walked closely beside me. I tried to compose myself, but I wept with more intensity than I have ever cried before. People watched with concerned eyes as I left a trail of tears through the hall of the hospital and I felt no shame. My outburst of emotion felt justified. The pain demanded to be seen and heard. My baby would never come home with me and I felt as if no one else could possibly understand the excruciating pain that accompanied that realization.

Driving away from the hospital tormented every maternal instinct within me. I knew Ethan's body was an empty shell and his soul was no longer there, but it was difficult to wrap my mind around it. I felt as if I were abandoning my infant child, cold and alone with no one to hold him.

Coming home was painful. Home was filled with memories that had never taken place. *Ethan was going to play in that yard. I was going to sing Ethan lullabies in that nursery. Chris was going to read Ethan stories on that chair. Ethan was going to come toddling down that hallway, his hair a mess, and watch cartoons on that television.*

When we arrived home, Chris helped me out of the car and into the house. I looked around and surveyed our cozy home. My mom had come the day before to clean for us. She had washed the dishes, vacuumed the floors, changed our sheets, and done the laundry. Everything was clean and organized. I should have felt relieved to be home, but I felt an ache deep inside. Something about our house did not feel like home. Someone was missing.

I slowly eased my body onto the couch, my incision still very tender from surgery. Chris walked down the hall and gently shut the door to Ethan's completed nursery. I thought back on the day Chris painted Ethan's room and the day he assembled his crib. I thought back on the time we sat in his room, marveling at the completed product. We dreamed about what it would be like for him to grow up in that space. What songs would we sing to him at night? What books would we read? How many times would we find him playing when he should have been sleeping? We had carefully selected and hung his woodland-themed wall decor. His room was perfect. It was as if the closed door was a cork on a bottle of wine. The door sealed in the laughter, the smiles, and the dreams we made in that room. Of course, I knew the idyllic feelings associated with his room would eventually escape. Ethan would never sleep in this room. He would not grow up here. The realization hit me hard. He would never come home to us. Chris returned to the living room, sat beside me and squeezed my hand. I leaned against him and allowed the tears to freely fall.

Later that night, my milk came in. My doctor had warned me this would happen soon and my breasts had felt tender and swollen all day. When I changed my shirt that evening, I noticed I had leaked through the tight sports bra I was wearing. I was so angry with my body. It felt cruel that my body thought Ethan was with us when my heart knew all too well he was gone.

I felt so broken, so wounded, and so incomplete. Everything ached, both physically and emotionally. It felt as if a part of my heart had been removed. Yet somehow I knew I would have done it again and again just to have another hour with him. Somehow it was still worth it.

Seven

Essential community

Our family and friends jumped in to help us during our first weeks at home. There is a quote from C.S. Lewis's *A Grief Observed* that best describes how we felt in those initial days. As Lewis reflects on the deep grief he experienced after the death of his wife, he writes, "I see people, as they approach me, trying to make up their minds whether they'll 'say something about it' or not. I hate if they do, and if they don't."[1] Amen to that.

Our community jumped in to help us during our first weeks at home. Our church arranged for someone to bring us a meal each evening. Close friends and family stopped by to keep us company. The support was encouraging on most days, but on some days it felt overwhelming. There were days when Chris and I would turn down an offer for help or an invitation for company simply because we felt too exhausted to navigate the minefield of small talk and questions. I hated to be alone, yet I dreaded the hurtful things people unknowingly say. As Lewis says, I hated it if they did and I hated it if they didn't. People say the darnedest things.

---

1. C.S. Lewis. *A Grief Observed.* (New York:Harper Collins, 1961), 10.

Kristin Hernandez

It did not take long for me to notice people tended to respond to our situation in one of three ways. The first group were the fixers, who did their best to fix our sadness by imparting some sort of wisdom or advice. I knew these statements were well intended, but they were often hurtful in the moment. It was the worst when the words weren't even true.

"Oh, don't cry. You should be happy Ethan is rejoicing in heaven." Someone said this to me and I felt bothered by how much the statement bothered me. I knew Ethan was no longer suffering. I knew my greatest pain was Ethan's greatest joy. I truly believe this and took comfort in that truth, but it was the way the words were said that bothered me. Like my tears were unwarranted. Like grief meant I didn't believe. Like a Band-Aid on a bullet wound.

"God must've needed him." I knew this wasn't true. God is sovereign over the entire universe. Does God really "need" anything? Is God really sitting there feeling like He can't accomplish His plan because Ethan was on Earth? There are a whole lot of holes in this statement, but I'd imagine we are all in agreement that this is a lie.

"He was too beautiful for earth." This one really made me scratch my head. There is no solid reasoning behind it and it also implies that all of us still walking around the earth are pretty ugly. I guess this one makes me giggle a little.

Or the most hurtful: "You're young. You'll definitely have more children." I hated hearing this. Children aren't replaceable. Of course I desired more children, but did the people who said this not realize I held this baby in my arms and watched him die? I'd never dream of sitting beside a friend who lost a spouse and saying, "Don't worry, you can get married again."

The second group, the "tiptoers," crept around us as if we were two grenades just waiting to explode. They were afraid to ask how we were doing or to mention Ethan's name for fear we would completely crumble. They avoided eye contact. They did their best to love us at arm's length. Now I didn't just feel heartbroken, I also felt socially awkward. No one wants to make people squirm and search for the nearest exit.

The third type of response was rare but refreshing. A select group of people knew how to simply be there for us without having to fix the situation. They asked questions and they asked us about Ethan. They let us talk about him. They offered to help. They admitted when they didn't know what to say. They kept us company when we needed it, but also knew how to graciously give us space. Many of them even spoke scripture and words of wisdom to us, but they did it all through tears and an acknowledgment of our pain. They loved us from the muddy trenches of grief, rather than at an arm's length.

I found all three of these reactions within the church. When I say "the church," I'm not referring to a particular congregation or building. I mean the collective body of Christian believers who make up the global church, or more specifically in this case, the American church. I mentioned before that church was difficult for me during my pregnancy with Ethan and those feelings didn't change after his birth. In fact, being around the church felt even more challenging. While my unbelieving friends were often the first to acknowledge the trauma of what we had been through, those within the church were more likely to diminish our pain with optimistic platitudes and advice about how we should feel. Living in community can feel messy and uncomfortable. And when we're grieving and our hearts are particularly broken, loving attempts from our friends and family to encourage us can feel downright painful.

It could be easy to look at the first two groups and allow bitterness to grow in my heart, but the truth is I *needed* those people. I needed the church. Those who unknowingly spoke hurtful sayings didn't know what to say. Those who tiptoed around us wanted to protect us from the pain. While it was good for me to gently and lovingly correct untruths and help my friends understand what I needed, it was just as important for me to extend grace. The same grace I needed as I navigated this too.

Community is essential. The Bible makes clear that God created us with the desire to be in community with one another. From Genesis 2:18, when God declared it was not good for Adam to be alone and created Eve, to Revelation, when God's children from every tribe, tongue, and nation worship together, and so many places in between, scripture shows the importance of community, particularly the community of the church, the Bride of Christ. 1 Corinthians 12:12–27 describes the church as one body with many parts, all baptized by one Holy Spirit, each created with different gifts, each of equal importance to the body. Even Jesus lived life in community with His twelve disciples and on the night before He would die, He asked His friends to stay with Him while he prayed (Mark 14:32–34). Even when it comes to addressing conflict within the church community, Matthew 18:20 says, "For where two or three are gathered in my name, there am I among them." I could go on and on with examples. We were created to live in community and I am grateful for the church, who showed Christ's love to me in tangible ways.

A story in Exodus 17:8–13 paints a stunning picture of the body of believers lifting each other up in a crisis.

Then Amalek came and fought with Israel at Rephidim. So Moses said to Joshua, "Choose for us men, and go out and fight with Amalek. Tomorrow I will stand on the top of the hill with the staff of God in my hand." So Joshua did as Moses told him, and fought with Amalek, while Moses, Aaron, and Hur went up to the top of the hill. Whenever Moses held up his hand, Israel prevailed, and whenever he lowered his hand, Amalek prevailed. But Moses' hands grew weary, so they took a stone and put it under him, and he sat on it, while Aaron and Hur held up his hands, one on one side, and the other on the other side. So his hands were steady until the going down of the sun. And Joshua overwhelmed Amalek and his people with the sword.

I want to be careful not to add meaning to this story, as I believe it was written about a specific people (the Israelites) to show God's favor toward His people. However, I do think we can look at this account and be encouraged by the way Moses's friends lifted him up when he needed help. I feel this way so often, yet I'm often slow to admit it. I need the church to come alongside me and "lift my arms" when I'm far too weary to go on. I need people to sit with me in my pain. I need people to lovingly speak truth to me when I lose my focus. I need my brothers and sisters to pray for me when I can't find the words.

Yes, hurtful things were said to me and the words stung. Some stopped speaking altogether. I was hurt and some of those wounds still throb when I dwell on the ways friends and family didn't live up to my expectations. And while I think it is okay and even good to acknowledge this, I needed to realize the horrible tragedy we had been through was not a free pass to withhold forgiveness from those around me. I needed to extend an outpouring of grace and forgiveness to the people around me. Heck, I needed an outpouring of grace and forgiveness myself.

Individualism is hailed as a value in our society and it's tempting for me to believe I don't need anyone else. I tell myself I'm strong and capable. I tell myself no one understands me and I can't expect them to. I don't need anyone else. But God didn't create us to operate as individuals. He created us for communion with one another. Christ loves the church. The church is His bride. He cherishes and nourishes it (Ephesians 5:29). He gave Himself for the church. As much as I wanted to pull away, I knew I wasn't created to do this alone. I was created to live in fellowship with the body, and when one part hurts, we all hurt together (1 Corinthians 12:26).

Eight

A celebration of life

Planning a funeral is never a pleasant experience, but it felt especially cruel and unnatural to be thrust into the process when we should have been sending birth announcements. It was a time when we should have been exhausted from sleepless nights soothing a crying baby, rather than sleepless nights of weeping and vivid nightmares. As much as I hated the thought of it, I also welcomed the distraction.

Planning a funeral felt like shopping for a used car you never wanted to buy. My heart and C-section incision both throbbed with each step to view another burial plot and each time I lowered myself into another funeral director's chair. The first location we visited (not the one we ended up choosing) left such a bitter taste in my mouth. The lobby of the cemetery's main building reminded me of a hotel. Ornate lights hung from the ceiling and plush pillows sat upon an assortment of large couches. A buffet table stood to the side, with cookies, coffee, and fruit-infused water for guests. The funeral director's beautifully decorated office felt out of place in the midst of such unpleasant circumstances. The funeral director was smooth and persuasive as she listed all of the upgrades we could purchase to give Ethan the "best" burial and to ultimately show our love for him. I knew immediately we were just another sale to her. She was preying on our vulnerable, grieving hearts and the whole experience made me want to vomit.

We visited two cemeteries before settling on one not too far from our home, in the town where I grew up. The staff spoke to us with such dignity and care, and the cemetery offered a significant discount for the burial of children. We knew this was the right place. We designed a headstone, putting careful thought into the words that would mark our son's legacy.

Chris and I decided early on we wanted to privately bury Ethan without any sort of graveside service, but we did want our friends and family to have the opportunity to remember him with us at a larger, public memorial service at our church. We were the only people other than our medical team who met Ethan while he was still alive. We saw his service as an opportunity to introduce our son to our friends and family and to share about the impact he had left on our lives. We hoped his life would continue to leave an impact on others. Throughout my pregnancy and in the days since Ethan's passing, many people asked us questions about our faith. They saw God's hand woven through Ethan's story and it intrigued them. We had been praying for months that Ethan's life would bring people to hope. We wanted to use this opportunity to share the reason for the hope we have: Jesus.

"I want to speak," I told Chris, as we discussed ideas for Ethan's service. "Maybe we can speak together. We knew him. No one else knew him. I want to introduce him to people."

Chris nodded and agreed we should both speak at Ethan's service. I set to work writing a eulogy, while Chris assembled a musical slideshow of photographs and video clips of Ethan's short life. We had taken many pictures throughout the pregnancy and at the birth.

We planned Ethan's memorial service for Saturday, August 29, nearly two weeks after we said goodbye. We met with our pastor the week before to finalize the plans. We knew it would be a sad day and tears would be shed, but we wanted people to leave feeling hope in the middle of the sorrow. Our pastor would share a gospel message, my dad would share a few words, Chris and I would share a eulogy, and the service would end with our photo slideshow.

We also planned a dessert reception in the multipurpose room. We wanted the reception to feel joyful, as if we were celebrating Ethan's life and his eternal homecoming. Cake and ice cream were a must for the menu.

Ethan's memorial service was something I anticipated with both dread and excitement. It sounds so strange to say out loud because it was a horrible time in my life, but I truly looked forward to celebrating our sweet baby's life and seeing all of our friends and family together. When you don't have your children with you, other events and milestones take on new meaning. When I couldn't invite friends over to meet him or dream about his first birthday, I put my energy into his memorial. Yet at the same time, I dreaded having to make small talk with so many people. What would people say? What if someone said something unintentionally hurtful? No matter how many times I had heard these comments in the past two weeks, hearing them still hurt. Would I be able to extend grace to people? Could I hold it together or would I sob throughout the entire service?

I began to pray for peace and for joy. Praying was hard after the way our hearts had been crushed by Ethan's passing, but a part of me still felt compelled to continue asking. *Lord, please help Chris and I get through this day. Calm our hearts. Give us the strength to speak on stage and the strength to speak to people after the service. Please give us your joy. Hold me together.*

Chris and I were struck with nerves on the morning of Ethan's service. I had tried to take my time getting ready, yet somehow found myself sitting on the couch completely dressed and ready an hour before we even needed to leave our house. My hair was curled, my makeup was done, and I wore the blue dress I had bought to wear at our baby shower that never took place. I nervously watched the clock tick, tick, tick, and counted down the minutes until we could get out of the house and get the service over with. My heart beat fast and I felt nauseous. *I don't know if I can do this.*

We arrived at the church about an hour before the service was set to begin. My nerves eased a bit as soon as I peeked into the multipurpose room where the reception was set to take place. Several women in our church had transformed the large room into an adorable forest-themed space. The decorations matched Ethan's nursery perfectly. Round tables covered with blue tablecloths were set up around the room. Each table displayed a plant centerpiece and tiny acorns made out of chocolate kisses and wafer cookies. Buffet tables had been set up on the side of the room to serve lemonade, cake and ice cream. It was better than I could have hoped for.

In lieu of a guest book, friends had set up an "encouragement box." The box was placed on a table with a sign that read, "Please leave a note, prayer, verse or signature for

Kristin and Chris." Pieces of paper were placed near the box with a variety of pens. Guests could write us a note during the reception and place it inside the box for Chris and me to read later. I loved the idea.

The room was perfect and I felt relieved. Planning the details of the reception had felt overwhelming and I gladly handed planning off to the women who graciously offered to take the reins. I was so thankful for their help and incredibly encouraged by their selfless support.

My nerves quickly began to dissipate as friends and family arrived and greeted us with warm hugs. The church sanctuary was soon filled with loved ones we had not seen for months, even years. Almost everyone we loved dearly was under one roof for the first time since our wedding and, though this may sound strange to say out loud given the painful circumstances, the sight genuinely made me feel happy. I looked over at Chris and could tell he shared the peace I felt. As we took our seats in the front row of the sanctuary, I thanked God for the comfort and peace only He can give.

"I'd be happy if *half* this many people came to my funeral," Chris whispered into my ear. I scanned the room and saw every chair was filled. Ushers brought in extra chairs and began to set them up in the back, to make room for the people that still trickled in. Nearly two hundred and fifty people from various stages of my life had come to celebrate Ethan's. I felt so thankful for the community around us and so proud of our little boy. I squeezed Chris's hand. "Me too."

The sanctuary decor was simple yet lovely. A large wooden table stood at the front of the stage, displaying large floral arrangements, framed photographs of Ethan, decorative wood stumps, and an adorable stuffed fox from our baby registry.

Our pastor spoke about the emphasis Jesus placed on children as the greatest in the kingdom of heaven and the call to childlike faith. My dad spoke next, sharing about the promise of eternity for those who know Christ. Chris and I read the eulogy we had written the week before and had also published in the local newspaper. We thanked our friends and family for their love, support, and prayers. Next, we shared about our sweet baby boy—his big personality full of life from the beginning, constant kicks and jabs, the foods he demanded through my cravings, and the way he always held his hands up in ultrasounds like he was about to fight. We spoke of God's goodness to us, even when life doesn't feel good. We spoke of His steadfast grace and the way He transforms us when our circumstances don't change. Our pastor returned to the stage and shared the gospel with all two hundred and fifty people who filled the room, many of whom we had been praying over for years.

The service ended with the slideshow Chris had prepared. I rested my head on Chris's shoulder and allowed the tears to freely fall. We watched as photos flashed across the screen. Photos of my growing belly, photos of Ethan's nursery, a video clip of me waving to the camera after I was admitted to Labor and Delivery, a video clip of the moment Ethan was born and, finally, photos of Ethan. Ethan with Chris. Ethan with me. Our family of three. Ethan's sweet face. It did not matter how many times we had seen the slideshow in the days before. Hot tears poured from my eyes.

The reception felt like a small glimpse of heaven. As I surveyed the room, I saw joy. People enjoyed sweet treats while visiting with one another. Friends laughed as they greeted one another and exchanged hugs. People smiled as they wrote notes of encouragement to place in our box. The room was brightly lit and lively, a beautiful contrast to the dim lighting and lament of the service. This was the exact atmosphere we had hoped for. It truly felt like a celebration of Ethan's short but impactful life. It felt like a reunion. It felt like home.

In the ninety-three minutes Ethan was alive, he had managed to make an impact on many lives. God has used his life to bring two hundred and fifty people together to hear about Jesus. Ethan accomplished more in his short life than some adults do in ninety years. I could not help but feel proud of our son.

Nine

Death and the grave

"Hi," a small voice said. I looked down and saw a small boy, about seven or eight, observing the room alongside me as people milled about the reception area. I had seen him at church before, but did not remember his name.

"Hi," I said back, offering a smile.

"That was sad," he said. He did not seem emotionally affected. He spoke directly with childlike honesty. He described what I had been feeling in such simple terms.

"You're right, it was sad," I said softly. "But you know what? It's sad for us, but it's very happy for Ethan. He is with Jesus and he is so happy."

The boy seemed to consider my words for a moment. "Do you miss him?" he asked.

I took a deep breath, fighting to hold back a tear. "Oh yes, I miss him a lot," I admitted honestly. "But I know I will see him again one day and that brings me comfort."

The young boy continued to ask me questions. He asked questions about heaven, questions about Ethan and questions about my feelings. All morning I had been nervous to see what kind of questions guests would ask me at the reception. I had expected these questions to come from adults, not from an innocent child. The little boy scampered away, seemingly content with my attempts to provide an answer to each of his questions, and I wondered why most adults are so afraid to talk about death.

I've thought about this a lot since that day–common reactions to death, even within the church. One common way of reacting to death is avoidance. Death is something all of us will face one day, yet so many of us tiptoe around the subject. We speak about the deceased in somber tones, practically whispering their names. We read up on the best diets, exercise routines, supplements, and life hacks to give ourselves the best shot at a long life. Death is something many of us fear, whether in conversation or in the form of it happening to those we love (or even to ourselves).

I've observed a second way many people respond to death, especially within the church, and that is a relaxed view that almost appears thoughtless. It is an approach that looks at a horrific death and is quick to say, "We should rejoice because they're in heaven. Don't cry. Celebrate. We can be happy because they aren't in pain." I believe in heaven. I believe in the promise of redemption and eternal life for those who believe in Jesus. I wholeheartedly believe we can rejoice in this assurance, but is there any room to lament? Can we view death as a horrendous curse Jesus came to defeat, while simultaneously rejoicing in the unshakeable hope we have as believers?

The day between Good Friday when Jesus was crucified and Easter Sunday when He victoriously rose from the dead is often referred to as Holy Saturday. It is a day of mourning and lament, even for those who cling tightly to the assurance that a glorious Sunday is coming. It often felt like many around me were trying to rush through our Holy Saturday to get to Sunday. Honestly, I think I wanted to rush through it too. The darkness of Saturday can feel so heavy and I'd much rather laugh than weep.

As I watch the news and consider the world around me, it seems as if most of us are living in some sort of "Holy Saturday" season. Pain and sorrow have come throughout our lives and we ache for peace. We long for all that is broken to be mended. We yearn for the day when every tear will be wiped from our eyes. As believers in Jesus, we know Resurrection Sunday has already happened and we rejoice in this incredible gift. We know this miracle means we too will have resurrection of our earthly bodies one day and Christ will return again to make all things new. We can shout for joy and praise God for our redemption through Christ and the assurance of eternity with Him. And as we do this, we can make space to recognize death for what it is: a horrible curse Jesus came to destroy. Something worth grieving as we keep our eyes focused on a Hope worth clinging to.

One of my close friends shared a quote with me from Pete Greig's book *God on Mute* that sums this up so well. Greig wrote about a funeral he attended for a friend who died suddenly, leaving his family behind. His Christian funeral was filled with encouraging songs, Scripture readings, and speeches. While I believe Christian funerals are truly celebrations, something he said deeply resonated with me. After observing his deceased friend's young daughter staring at her father's casket, he writes:

In spite of all the singing, dancing and detailed assurances (or perhaps because of them), I drove away later thinking how very fragile our faith must be if we can't just remain sad, scared, confused and doubting for a while. In our fear of unknowing, we leapfrog Holy Saturday and rush the resurrection. We race disconcerted to make meaning and find beauty where there is simply none. Yet. From dusk on Good Friday to dawn on Easter Sunday, God allowed the whole of creation to remain in a state of chaos and despair.[2]

It doesn't feel good to mourn over the grave, but perhaps God gave us an intentional space to reflect, lament, and turn to Him with our pain. We can certainly rejoice in the truth that this world is not our own and eternal joy is ahead for those who are in Christ, and we can cry out in pain over the brokenness of today.

I wonder if many of us try to brush aside the topic of death because we discredit the worth of our temporary earthly bodies. Christ has promised a new, perfect resurrected body for those who believe in Him and this causes me to approach death with hope and confidence. Continuing to bear this in mind, God created us in His own image and called that creation "good" (Genesis 1:26, 31). Psalm 139:13 says He knit us together and we are fearfully and wonderfully made. Our temporary bodies are not our eternal home, but each precious one was made with care.

Ethan's death pushed me to truly consider what I believe about eternity. I hate to admit how attached my heart has been to this earth when an indescribable gift waits for those who call upon the name of Jesus. Death is inevitable and this world is not my final destination. Philippians 3:20–21

2. Greig, Pete. *God on Mute: Engaging the Silence of Unanswered Prayer.* (Grand Rapids: Baker Books, 2007), 202.

says, "But our citizenship is in heaven, and from it we await a Savior, the Lord Jesus Christ, who will transform our lowly body to be like his glorious body, by the power that enables him even to subject all things to himself."

Jesus talked about eternity over and over while He was on earth. He came as an atonement for our sins so we could enter into His kingdom if we put our trust in Him. Jesus told His disciples in John 14:3, "And if I go and prepare a place for you, I will come again and will take you to myself, that where I am you may be also." Our home is with Him.

In 2 Corinthians 4:17, Paul writes, "For this light momentary affliction is preparing for us an eternal weight of glory beyond all comparison." Ethan's death did not feel light or momentary. The pain felt heavy and damaging. At first, it was difficult to see beyond the pain. In time, I began to realize this life is merely a vapor.

I remember asking my father about eternity when I was a little girl. "Daddy, how long is forever?" My father considered the question for a moment before motioning to the long stretch of highway ahead of us. "Do you see that, honey?" he asked. "Do you see how far this road goes?" I nodded, looking at the miles stretched out in front of us. "Imagine this road is eternity. Our life is just a small dot on the road. Compared to the entire highway, this dot is so small. In the span of eternity, it feels like a quick blink of your eye." That analogy has stuck with me for years. This small little "dot" of a life felt so painful, yet it did not compare to the treasure that waits for me in eternity with Jesus. In 1 Corinthians 2:9, Paul says "But, as it is written, 'What no eye has seen, nor ear heard, nor the heart of man imagined, what God has prepared for those who love him.'"

I began to realize the ache in my heart was not simply for Ethan. Yes, I wanted to see Ethan so badly. Yes, I missed him with every breath in my body. But in the midst of that yearning, I began to yearn for something more. My heart yearned for Jesus. I yearned for home. 2 Corinthians 5:1-10 says:

> For we know that if the tent that is our earthly home is destroyed, we have a building from God, a house not made with hands, eternal in the heavens. For in this tent we groan, longing to put on our heavenly dwelling, if indeed by putting it on we may not be found naked. For while we are still in this tent, we groan, being burdened—not that we would be unclothed, but that we would be further clothed, so that what is mortal may be swallowed up by life. He who has prepared us for this very thing is God, who has given us the Spirit as a guarantee. So we are always of good courage. We know that while we are at home in the body we are away from the Lord, for we walk by faith, not by sight. Yes, we are of good courage, and we would rather be away from the body and at home with the Lord. So whether we are at home or away, we make it our aim to please him. For we must all appear before the judgment seat of Christ, so that each one may receive what is due for what he has done in the body, whether good or evil.

Matthew 6:19-21 says, "Do not lay up for yourselves treasures on earth, where moth and rust destroy and where thieves break in and steal, but lay up for yourselves treasures in heaven, where neither moth nor rust destroys and where thieves do not break in and steal. For where your treasure is, there your heart will be also." For years, I had been building storehouses on earth. I placed my happiness and my feelings of comfort on my education, my job, and my husband. Now don't get me wrong. It's quite alright to have these things. My problem was these items were where I was placing my hope and my well-being. I was not looking to God for comfort in the ways I should have.

As I wrestled with God and sought truth, my perspective began to shift. I was the one who had not yet made it home. Ethan was already home. He was already home with the Lord, free from pain or tears. My greatest pain was his greatest joy.

So I weep at my son's grave knowing death is not the end, just as Jesus wept over the death of His dear friend Lazarus knowing He would again raise him up (John 11). Death is inevitable, but the grave holds no power over Jesus. His resurrection signified the death of death and His second coming will bring this to completion. The death of death is an incredible thing to ponder. When I think on this, I can't help but rejoice knowing our God knows our suffering even better than we do and came to abolish the very thing that has brought us the most pain.

Jesus is coming back one day to conquer death and sadness once and for all.

Revelation 21:4 says, "He will wipe away every tear from their eyes, and death shall be no more, neither shall there be mourning, nor crying, nor pain anymore, for the former things have passed away." In the meantime he tells us, "In the world you will have tribulation. But take heart; I have overcome the world" (John 16:33). He knows this world will be filled with pain and suffering. While he does not condemn us for our tears, he encourages us to take heart and cling to the truth that he has overcome this broken world.

I can't describe the peace we felt as we drove away from Ethan's memorial service that afternoon. Chris squeezed my hand as we drove home and we both exhaled a sigh of relief. I look back now and see that it may seem like a bizarre choice following a difficult day, but we spontaneously went out to dinner that night with some of our closest friends who had come into town for the service. The day wrapped up with fits of laughter and frozen custard on the patio of our favorite ice cream spot. I felt so thankful for our friends, who had supported us so well over the past few months. It felt good to laugh when my eyes felt weary from so much weeping. It felt even better to remember all Christ has done for us and the hope we have in Him. To rejoice through tearful eyes.

Ten

You hold it all

E ven in the earliest hours of grief, my heart yearned to be pregnant again. I fully understood another baby would never replace Ethan and any future pregnancies were not guaranteed to be without complications. I had been given a taste of motherhood, even if only for a few hours, and I was willing to face whatever risks may come to have that feeling again, even if only for a moment.

"I'd do it again," I told Chris while we were still in the postpartum unit. "As soon as my doctor says it's okay, I think we should try again." Chris sat on the edge of my hospital bed, tears in his eyes, and shook his head. "I can't ever watch you go through this again."

I knew this wasn't a decision to rush. We had both been thrust into the depths of grief and it would take time to learn how to communicate and support one another as we mourned in our own unique ways. God would certainly have provided if we had become pregnant sooner, but I don't think we were ready to bring a baby home in those first few months. God used this time to work in our broken hearts and in our marriage. My doctors had told me I needed to take some time to heal physically before putting my body through the challenges of pregnancy, and the timeline relieved some of the pressure to have a plan for our future attempts to expand our family.

One month after Ethan's passing, Chris and I returned to the genetic counselor's office. I sank into the padded chair and soaked in my surroundings. My thoughts went back to that horrible day in June when we had first learned Ethan was going to have to fight for his life. The memory was vivid. I remembered the way the geneticist softly explained the defects in Ethan's brain and heart, and how her sweet tone could not soften the blow to my heart. I remembered how helpless I felt as she offered various testing and presented our "options."

I thought back on everything that had happened since our last visit, just three months prior. I felt different. Older, somehow.

As the geneticist spoke, I felt much more level-headed than I had been at our last visit. However, I was anxious to receive answers. Testing had been done on Ethan's cord blood and I was hopeful we would learn more about his condition. I took a deep breath and braced myself for any words the genetic counselor may say next.

"Your son had Full Trisomy 9," she said, revealing the mystery I had been waiting months to discover. "Not only is Trisomy 9 rare, but to have been born alive with *Full* Trisomy 9 is surprising." The genetic counselor explained Ethan had three instances of the ninth chromosome in every cell of his body. Humans usually have twenty-three pairs of chromosomes. Sometimes, a third copy of a particular chromosome will be present. This results in a trisomy. The most common trisomy is Trisomy 21, more commonly known as Down syndrome. Unlike Down syndrome, Full Trisomy 9 is always fatal.

The geneticist continued to explain the way that chromosomes are formed as cells begin to split at conception. As she spoke, I was struck with awe at the complexity of life. Every single cell and every piece of DNA must form perfectly in order for someone to live. One small anomaly along the way could result in the inability to live. The simple fact that I am alive no longer seemed so simple. Life suddenly felt incredibly miraculous. I pondered my life as well as Ethan's. None of this could have been a mistake. His life, though short, was strategically designed.

That same day we met with one of the NICU doctors who had been present at Ethan's birth. She had seen the official autopsy and asked if we would like to meet to review what had been found. As we spoke, she confirmed the rarity of Ethan's condition. He was the only baby she had ever seen born alive with Full Trisomy 9.

It was obvious to me Ethan was a miracle. The rarity of Ethan's condition was confirmed over and over. The doctor seemed so surprised that Ethan, a baby with Full Trisomy 9, made it to the third trimester and was born alive. The spontaneous nature of his condition, along with its rarity, proved to me that God had a purpose for this anomaly. He had been handpicked to carry out a specific purpose in the ninety-three minutes we had him. He had already beaten the odds.

We had begged and pleaded with God for a child and He answered. We prayed from day one God would use Ethan's life to bring people to know Jesus and He answered. We prayed God would protect Ethan in the womb and He answered. We prayed God would give me a smooth delivery and He did. We prayed God would give us the opportunity to meet our son and He did. Not only this, but He gave us ninety-three minutes with him. With a one-in-a-million baby that should have naturally miscarried.

We prayed God would allow Ethan to come home with us and He said no. One no in a sea of yeses. One no that provided Ethan with much more than we could have ever offered him. Ethan will not come to us, but we will one day go to him.

I felt calm as we left the hospital. Oh, my heart still longed for Ethan, but I felt so much peace. I was beginning to see God's hand in every detail of his short life. He had been here against all odds. His life had purpose.

"What are the odds of this happening again?" Chris asked.

"Very low," the geneticist assured him. The geneticist presented statistics and explained Ethan's condition was not something we could have genetically passed down to him. "This was simply a spontaneous occurrence and I have no concerns of this happening again."

Our grieving hearts were soothed by this news. We carefully considered our hearts, our mental health, and the advice our doctors had given us. We were grieving, but had both started to find joy in everyday events and the timing felt right. We were terrified, yet hopeful to grow our family. About six months after Ethan's passing, we decided to pursue another pregnancy with both caution and hope.

We had struggled for so long to get pregnant with Ethan and I never expected it to only take a month to conceive. As I stared down at the positive pregnancy test, I felt hesitation instead of pure joy. I walked into the kitchen, where Chris was packing his lunch for the workday.

"Well, I'm pregnant," I said calmly, handing him the test.

His reaction was grateful, yet somber. He wrapped me in a hug and we simply stood there for a few moments, soaking in the sacred reality of what we had just discovered. We were hopeful yet nervous. We both knew we weren't promised a smooth pregnancy and there were no guarantees of anything. We knew this baby might not come home with us, but we prayed he or she would. We prayed for protection over this little life and that God would allow us to raise this child.

I started bleeding less than a week later.

I sat in the same ER where I had gone after experiencing spotting with Ethan, but this time everything felt different. The optimism and innocence I had carried a year before had been replaced with a firsthand understanding that innocent babies die.

A doctor soon confirmed what I already knew. Our baby was gone. I didn't cry at first. As the doctor spoke the words to me, I felt numb. I also felt tired. I felt tired of crying, tired of grieving, and tired of heartache. I laid in the hospital bed and took a slow, deep breath. I waited for the sobs to shake my body, but nothing came. I hated that. How could my heart ache so deeply yet no tears flow? How could I not cry out in agony? How could I just sit here in silence when my second child had died?

God, what now? Why us? Why again?

I didn't understand. Why would God, in all of His power, allow us to lose not just one, but two babies?

I knew God is sovereign. I knew He would take care of us. He had proven time and time again He would provide for us. But I wrestled with Him and shook my fist at the sky. I felt angry and betrayed. This was supposed to be the redemptive ending to our heartbreaking story.

It only took about a week for my hCG levels to drop back to the normal range, confirming my body was no longer pregnant. I followed up with a doctor a week later and she confirmed my body was responding "wonderfully"—an ironic word for something so awful.

My doctor recommended we wait two months before pursuing another pregnancy and Chris and I eagerly began to try again as soon as the recommended time had passed. I discovered I was pregnant for the third time on the morning of Ethan's first birthday. The day was already bound to be emotional, and this unexpected news only added to the onslaught of feelings that filled my heart. I was so happy to be pregnant again, yet my heart ached with guilt that I had allowed this discovery to overshadow Ethan's first birthday. But perhaps this was it and the timing was significant. Perhaps God had carried us through this difficult season to draw us closer to Him, and would now grant us the desire of our heart. Maybe God was working yet another miracle in our lives by providing a child to us on the anniversary of the birth and death of our first.

As the days went on, I slowly allowed my heart to fill with hope. I found myself singing in the kitchen and dreaming of the future. The timing felt right. Things were finally starting to come together. Through it all, I prayed for God's will in our lives and in the life of our child. I could feel Him continuing to refine my heart to completely surrender my dreams and to fully trust in Him.

A few weeks later I began to experience some physical pain, which I chalked up to paranoia. No matter how much I tried to distract myself and push these feelings aside, the aches and sharp twinges intensified until I finally called my doctor's office in the middle of the workday. A nurse with a calming demeanor asked me a series of questions—if I was bleeding, how painful the sensation was—and recommended I stop by the hospital for an ultrasound that afternoon.

My hands trembled as I gripped the steering wheel and drove to the hospital that held so many bittersweet memories. Flashbacks came at me as I caught a glimpse of the buildings and exited the freeway.

"Lord, give me strength to step onto this property," I whispered with a shaky voice.

My music library had been on shuffle and I noticed the song "You Hold It All" by Travis Ryan playing softly through my car speakers.

From the highest of mountains
To the depths of the sea
From the planets in motion
To the breath that we breathe
From the womb of the barren
To the rich and the poor
To the dreams of the orphan
Every heartbeat is Yours
You hold it all
You hold it all
You hold it all
You hold it all[3]

I let the words wash over me as I sat in the parking structure. I took a deep breath, almost as if to soak in the truth of the lyrics. As I exhaled, I felt my racing heart begin to slow to a steady pace. "God, thank you for holding it all.

---

3. Ryan, Travis. You Hold It All. Integrity Music, 2015, Accessed April 4, 2021. https://open.spotify.com/album/5amuOHLU6V7ktXtq3Apl4c.

Thank you for being sovereign in every breath and in every heartbeat. Please give me peace."

I recited these lyrics to myself over and over, almost as if to convince my broken heart to cling to what was true.

"I'm not seeing any sign of an embryo," the doctor said in a calm, steady voice.

From the womb of the barren...

"...possibly something we call a blighted ovum."

Every heartbeat is Yours ...

"...I'd like to order a few blood tests to see if your pregnancy hormones are rising or falling..."

You hold it all.

Chris and I returned to the hospital the following week for an ultrasound and additional blood work. My blood tests had shown significant hCG levels confirming pregnancy, but they were lower than the doctor would have expected to see at that gestational stage. I was instructed to stop by the laboratory every other day to have my blood drawn so the doctor could see whether my hormones were rising or falling.

I closed my eyes as yet another technician performed yet another ultrasound. I'd imagine many mothers feel excitement with each chance to catch a glimpse of their unborn baby on the screen, but ultrasounds became very triggering and traumatic for me (and still are something I struggle with). I took a deep breath and sang the words silently to myself.

> *From the womb of the barren*
> *To the rich and the poor*
> *To the dreams of the orphan*
> *Every heartbeat is Yours.*

The ultrasound only brought more difficult news. There was no sign of an embryo. I continued to have my blood drawn every two days until the hormone levels eventually stopped increasing. I finally miscarried a week later. "Finally" is another ironic word to use in this scenario. I never would have chosen to lose this pregnancy, yet I felt a sense of relief for all of the unknowns, phlebotomy needles, and ultrasounds to be behind us. We were finally able to rest in the rubble of what had once been a dream. Losing our third child ripped open the wound of shame, inadequacy, and feelings of abandonment.

After our third loss, my ob-gyn suggested Chris and I undergo a few routine tests to search for a potential underlying cause to my recurrent miscarriages. Once again we were assured my miscarriages were not likely related to Ethan's condition. Every doctor we had spoken with seemed convinced Ethan's diagnosis was a once-in-a-lifetime anomaly.

I was tested for a variety of blood-clotting disorders, which can lead to recurrent miscarriages, but each test came back normal. The next step was for Chris and I to both undergo karyotype testing. A karyotype test, or chromosome analysis, evaluates the number, structure, and size of your chromosomes to determine if you are a carrier for a variety of genetic problems. The test requires a simple blood draw, but the results can feel anything but simple. I had a sinking feeling one of us was a carrier for a genetic abnormality. More specifically, I had a sinking feeling I was a carrier for a fatal abnormality. Why else would it have taken so long for us to conceive Ethan? Why else would all three of our children have died from suspected chromosomal abnormalities? I was convinced something was wrong with me and I hoped the test would provide us with clarity.

We received our results three weeks later. Both were normal. No chromosomal abnormalities on either side. For weeks, I had expected to receive difficult news and had braced myself for an abnormal genetic finding. Instead, I was met with reassuring news that didn't leave me feeling any more reassured than I had been before. I wanted an answer and instead had even more questions. *Why does this keep happening?*

Chris and I set up a consultation with the Reproductive Endocrinology and Infertility department to review our history and to explore our options moving forward. The doctor, a kind and patient man who immediately made us feel at ease, reviewed our history and ordered a few additional tests and physical exams. We visited his office again a few weeks later to receive the results.

I had developed PCOS–polycystic ovarian syndrome. Abnormal results from my blood tests and a quick scan of my ovaries clearly confirmed the diagnosis. The doctor went on to explain PCOS and what it may mean for my future. "Based on your history and your condition, I'd say you have about a 60 percent chance of loss each time you get pregnant," he stated. "It is possible to get pregnant, but it will be harder for you."

"I've had so many exams…How come no one ever told me?" I asked softly, tears welling up in my eyes again.

"It's very likely you didn't have cysts before," the doctor explained. "It's quite possible you've always had the condition, but the symptoms haven't manifested themselves until recently."

I allowed the tears to overflow from my eyes and drip down my face. It felt cruel to have a frustrating condition develop after all we had been through. It was as if salt were being rubbed into the three gaping wounds in my heart. Not only did I have to live without my babies, but I had developed an endocrine disorder during the process.

Chris and I were weary. We decided to take a break from pursuing pregnancy and to turn our attention to other things—church, community group, friendships, our jobs, each other. Months passed and our hearts began to feel lighter. I thrust myself into Bible studies, the exhilaration of a long run, and time with friends. Though the longing for children never went away, we truly began to find deep joy in other things. I felt authentic hope for a future that may not include another pregnancy.

I had avoided going to church on Mother's Day during the previous years, but that next spring felt different. I was pleasantly surprised that the thought of sitting beside beaming mothers and the possibility of sitting through a cheesy video on the joys of motherhood didn't feel traumatic to me. We decided to go.

Instead of clichés and over-the-top presentations, the theme that day was God's heart for adoption. Not just the earthly adoption of children, but the way we have been adopted as sons and daughters of God. The service concluded with words from two couples who had grown their families through foster care. Something stirred in my heart and I couldn't shake it all day.

"I want to do this," I told Chris later that evening, a bit hesitant and unsure of how he'd react.

"Me too," he said.

We dove headfirst into the process of becoming foster parents. We spoke with parents who had grown their families through foster care and adoption. We knew there would be challenges and the goal was to reunite children with their birth families. We fully accepted that the process would not be an easy one, yet we were both bursting with excited anticipation. We were ready. We quickly submitted our first application and received the date for our first meeting with our case worker.

A few days before our first meeting, I had a routine appointment with my ob-gyn to check up on my PCOS. I had been trying out a few natural remedies, such as tweaking my diet, and was feeling much better. The plan was to do a quick ultrasound to see if my cysts had improved.

You can imagine my shock when the doctor told me the cysts were completely gone and I was pregnant instead. Unlike any of our previous pregnancies, this one felt textbook normal. Weeks passed and my pregnancy hormones rose beautifully. I was plagued with morning sickness, which was both miserable and incredibly reassuring. Our first ultrasound revealed two wiggly babies and two healthy heartbeats. I was pregnant with identical twins.

The foster care agency we had applied with did not allow families to receive placements while they had an infant and we made the difficult decision to withdraw our application. I was surprised to feel upset at this sudden turn of events. I had become excited about fostering and didn't want to withdraw. As confusing as this change was, we also felt peace knowing this pregnancy was not the result of our own plans. We had prayed God would make it clear if we were not supposed to pursue fostering through this agency during this season, and He slammed the door shut.

We allowed ourselves to feel joy and excitement. The timing felt perfect, as if God was restoring all we had lost with a double portion. Chris and I were so hopeful we would be bringing two babies home at the end of this pregnancy. We researched double strollers. My morning sickness intensified, much to my relief. We had more appointments. There were still two heartbeats.

When I was nearly eleven weeks pregnant, I visited my ob-gyn for what was supposed to be an uneventful checkup. The doctor rolled the ultrasound wand over my belly and peered at the screen for a long time. I immediately knew something was wrong. Both babies lay perfectly still and I could not see the flicker of their hearts like I had before. I held my breath as the Doppler was switched on. I desperately hoped to hear the whooshing sound of our babies' hearts beating, but I was met by the sound of silence instead. I received a second opinion, which only confirmed what we already knew. Our miracle twins were gone and a D&C procedure was scheduled for the following day.

I felt as if I had been led into the desert to wander. Our plans had been derailed by a miracle that had been ripped away from us. I was angry. Wasn't there a better way to reroute us?

Whereas meeting Ethan was bittersweet, my miscarriages were only bitter. I grieved I knew nothing of these babies I loved so much. I never got to hold them. I don't know if they were boys or girls. The precious babies I had carried in my womb felt like strangers to me and I hated that. These losses, although different than the loss of Ethan, were incredibly painful and hurt me in ways losing Ethan hadn't. I didn't feel joy as I had when I first held Ethan. Losing those sweet little babies was only associated with feelings of pain and shame.

I welcomed opportunities to talk about Ethan and to share his story. I felt as if his life mattered. I saw how God used his story to bring others hope, and I saw how speaking of his life brought me hope. It was a sharp contrast to the silence and discouragement I felt regarding miscarriage. I held these babies close to my chest, near my heart. Miscarriage stirs up a lot of emotions, but the one that caught me by surprise was loneliness. Many who found out often brushed it aside as "common." "At least it was early," they'd say. Their words may have been true, but common or early does not make something less devastating. A loss is a loss. A life is a life. I often kept this experience to myself, carefully selecting those I could trust. What if other people thought something was wrong with me? What if they pitied me? People already treated me differently after we lost Ethan— how much more of a social outcast would I feel like now that I had lost four more babies? What if they were right and something was wrong with me? Am I not a good mother? How come I couldn't save them?

From the highest of mountains
To the depths of the sea
From the planets in motion
To the breath that we breathe

From the womb of the barren
To the rich and the poor
To the dreams of the orphan
Every heartbeat is Yours
You hold it all
You hold it all
You hold it all
You hold it all

Eleven

Wrestling and warfare

At times I felt as if God had led us out into the wilderness only to leave us there. I didn't understand why God would open my womb after years of infertility only for the first five of our long-awaited pregnancies to end with death. I felt abandoned, betrayed, and confused. I believed God is all-knowing and all-powerful. I never doubted His existence or His ability to heal our son, yet I questioned whether He was who I always thought He was. I especially doubted His love for me.

As I wrestled with feelings of abandonment, I also wrestled with feelings of guilt. Could I really be a Christian and battle such deep feelings of disappointment toward God? Shouldn't I have peace? Where was my faith?

Christians were especially difficult to be around. I was desperate to understand more about God and to draw near to Him. I craved strong theology and wanted to know everything the Bible had to say about suffering, eternity, doubt, salvation, and God's character. Jesus was all I had to cling to and I longed for Him. I wanted to be in church, but the unintentionally hurtful remarks from other believers made it difficult. I felt ashamed of my wrestling. I didn't realize the unhelpful comments that brought me so much pain were actually built on an incomplete understanding of scripture.

One Sunday morning not long after Ethan died, a church greeter welcomed me with a warm smile and asked how I was doing. Desiring support and sisterly encouragement, I was transparent with her. "Honestly, I'm having a really hard day today," I said, choking back tears. Instead of the encouragement I was hoping for, a bewildered look swept across her face. You would have thought I had given the most outlandish answer imaginable. "Oh honey, you'd better be better than that," she exclaimed, flashing a bright smile. "God is on the throne!"

I believed her. I believe God was on the throne then, just as He is now and just as He will be every day from now on. But her words, though true, didn't comfort me. As she quickly moved on to greeting the next person, I felt ashamed of my honest answer. Maybe I should keep this struggle to myself.

One Wednesday night, I began to cry as I asked for prayer. A woman patted me on the back and flashed a wide smile at me, seemingly unaware of the fat tears falling from my cheeks. "Don't cry," she chirped. "Just have faith!" I sniffed back my tears, longing for more faith and for someone to simply carry out the admonition in Romans 12:15 to "weep with those who weep."

I continued to wrestle through each sleepless night, anxiety attack, and flashback. My heart felt broken. I wanted to understand. I wanted to feel close to God. Nothing felt normal for us and I questioned everything. It was as if I had fallen to the ground and was stumbling to regain my footing as the world continued to move forward at rushing speeds, unaware of how much pain I was in. It was as if people were running past me, shouting in their best cheerleading voice, "Just get back up." Everything in me wanted to cry out, "I want to get back up, but my leg is broken! Please, slow down and help me! Show me how to walk again with a leg like this!" I hated the shame I felt for even having a broken leg in the first place. It was as if my grief and lament made me a lesser Christian.

Grief isn't sin. I knew this, but the responses and well-meaning phrases from Christians around me made me question whether my grief was sinful. The way people pressed me to "just be thankful" and to "just trust God" made me feel ashamed for my broken heart. Why did I have to feel gratitude and grief at the same time? Why did I experience confusion and trust at the same time? Why couldn't I "just be thankful and trusting"? As I searched the scriptures for guidance, I was surprised to find a lack of "just be thankful" types of responses. While I was certainly met with the exhortation to be grateful, rest in the work Christ did on the cross, and to keep my eyes fixed on the incredible hope we have of eternity with Jesus, it was often paired with an acknowledgment of the trials and tribulations of this world and an invitation to lament.

Throughout scripture, so many of God's people suffered, doubted, and asked questions. Their questions did not cause God to abandon them or to make Him question His love for them. Job lamented that it would have been better if he were never born. Joseph was sold into slavery by his brothers. Many of the disciples were martyred. David filled the book of Psalms with lament, agony, and questions. Psalm 22 opens with an anguished cry of "My God, my God, why have you forsaken me?" The author David is often referred to as "a man after God's own heart." David knew how to simultaneously praise and lament. Despite his questions, he praised God. He never stopped giving God glory, even in his pain. Despite his incredible faith, he still had questions and sorrow. His faith and his distress did not cancel each other out. God drew near to him as he cried out in distress. God didn't look at David and say, "Wow, you sure have a bad attitude. I'm going to choose someone else." God still set David apart to bring Him glory and to be a part of the lineage of Jesus.

Of all the examples of suffering and grief throughout the Bible, the greatest example can be found in Jesus Christ. The realization that Jesus is familiar with grief has brought me such comfort. Isaiah 53:3 says, "He was despised and rejected by men; a man of sorrows, and acquainted with grief." Jesus isn't described as a happy-go-lucky guy with a cheesy smile on his face. He isn't referred to as the life of the party or the person who tells the best jokes. He isn't one to tell us that tears are shameful or that we need to simply "think positive." Jesus is called a "man of many sorrows."

Jesus openly wept when His friend Lazarus died, despite knowing he would soon rise again (John 11:35). He recognized the horror of death, even temporary death for those who are in Christ. Jesus retreated to be alone when He heard about the death of John the Baptist (Matthew 14:13). Jesus doesn't only tell us it's okay to grieve. He goes even further to call those who mourn "blessed" (Matthew 5:4). Jesus was betrayed by one of His own disciples and was turned over to be killed in exchange for thirty pieces of silver (Matthew 26). He was despised and rejected. He suffered an excruciating death. He felt God turn His face away as He hung on the cross. Jesus knows any pain we can imagine.

On the night before He would be crucified, Jesus' soul was "overwhelmed with sorrow to the point of death" (Matthew 26:38 NIV). Jesus—God in the flesh—knew what the outcome would be. He knew of the incredible gift of salvation in Christ. He knew of eternity with the Father, free from pain, sorrow or tears. But despite this knowledge, He knew how horrific death is. He sweat droplets of blood as He pleaded with the Father for another way to bring salvation to His children. Yet as He lamented and grieved, He surrendered to God. "Not my will, but yours be done."

We have permission to grieve. We have permission to wail, to doubt, and to question. God can handle all of our questions and our hurts. We can bring all of that to Him, knowing "he has not despised or scorned the suffering of the afflicted one; he has not hidden his face from him but has listened to his cry for help" (Psalm 22:24).

Jesus knew just how awful death is, which is why He came to save us from it. It wasn't until I came face to face with the devastation of death that I began to truly understand the gospel. I grew up in the church and I was familiar with the Bible. I understood God created a perfect world and death and pain entered the world because of man's disobedience. I understood because God is perfect, He could no longer look upon man in his wretchedness. I understood payment was necessary to make things right. I understood the need for a sacrifice to atone for the sins of the world. I understood God sent His son Jesus—fully God yet fully man—to come to earth and to die a horrible death in our place. I understood Jesus took all of our sin on the cross and covered us so we could have a relationship with God. I understood Jesus rose from the dead, ascended to Heaven, and is coming back to earth one day to make all things right.

I could quote the scriptures and I believed them to be true, but it wasn't until I was left to sort through the aftermath of Ethan's death that the weight of the gospel began to flood through my heart. Jesus came to be the death of death, and to destroy it forever.

Because of the saving work of Jesus Christ, we do not grieve as the rest of the world—but this does not mean we do not grieve. Our grief, though still filled with lament and tears, looks wildly different. 1 Thessalonians 4:13–18 says:

> But we do not want you to be uninformed, brothers, about those who are asleep, that you may not grieve as others do who have no hope. For since we believe that Jesus died and rose again, even so, through Jesus, God will bring with him those who have fallen asleep. For this we declare to you by a word from the Lord, that we who are alive, who are left until the coming of the Lord, will not precede those who have fallen asleep. For the Lord himself will descend from heaven with a cry of command, with the voice of an archangel, and with the sound of the trumpet of God. And the dead in Christ will rise first. Then we who are alive, who are left, will be caught up together with them in the clouds to meet the Lord in the air, and so we will always be with the Lord. Therefore encourage one another with these words.

What a beautiful promise for those who are in Christ. We have so much to look forward to. We do not grieve as those who are hopeless. Yes, we grieve, we cry, we lament, and our hearts are heavy. But as our hearts ache, we know all that feels hopeless is not without hope. We know this incredible pain is not the end. We know good is coming, and this often causes us to wrestle as we await the day when every tear is wiped from our eyes.

Wrestling is intimate. It includes gripping on to God, even when we're hurting or angry. It includes asking hard questions, seeking truth in scripture, and coming to God with our difficult emotions, especially when those things don't come naturally. It takes faith to seek God when we're experiencing doubt. The process of wrestling requires faith that He hears us and faith that He is who He says He is, even when our emotions don't line up with what we know to be true. I believe God welcomes us to ask Him hard questions, and He is glorified when we turn to Him and seek His face.

Wrestling is different than walking away. I imagine a wrestling match in which one of the competitors steps onto the mat, looks their opponent in the eye, tosses some angry words at them, spins on their heels, and walks away. No one in the audience would call that a true wrestling match. The real action wouldn't begin until the same person reached forward and began to engage with the person in front of them. In this same way, wrestling with God is different than tossing angry words at Him and running away. When we wrestle with God, we bring Him our frustrations, our doubts, and our anger, but rather than run we continue to seek Him and engage with Him. We grip onto Him and His Word, pleading for truth as tears stream down our faces.

In my wrestling, I dug into scripture. At first, it was out of spite. I wanted to find a flaw. I wanted to understand why God would allow such pain. As I immersed myself in the Bible, my own misconceptions were exposed. I saw just how much scripture addressed suffering and the contrast of the incomparable treasure I have in Christ.

In my wrestling, I turned to God with honest prayer and lament. I told Him how angry I was. I brought Him my questions. I talked to Him about the parts of scripture that confused me. I told Him about my doubts and my desire for the truth. He didn't turn away. As I prayed, read the Bible, and sought out truth, the Holy Spirit continued to speak to my heart.

I repeated the process of wrestling over and over. Read. Pray. Seek counsel from trusted people in my church. Rest in the truth. Doubt. Read. Pray. Seek counsel. Repeat. It was a process I was afraid to engage in, but I found it incredibly intimate. I have never prayed so much as in my seasons of wrestling. On some days, I could not find any words to say. I would simply cry and ask the Holy Spirit to intercede for me. I would call out to Jesus, sometimes barely whispering His name. I hated how weak I felt, yet I loved how close I felt to God. I was desperate for Him. I knew I could not function without Him. This is true in all circumstances, but I have felt it the clearest in wrestling seasons.

In Genesis 32:22–32, Jacob wrestled with God. He grappled all night long, saying, "I will not let you go until you bless me." The wrestling match resulted in a limp and a new name, Israel, which means "he struggles with God." God gave Jacob this new name to signify he had wrestled with God and with others and had overcome. Jacob (Israel) went on to father God's chosen people and the lineage of Jesus.

While I welcome the process of wrestling, it is important for us to remember a spiritual battle wages all around us. The enemy doesn't play fair and will try to strike us at our weakest points. I would caution us to continue to cling to God as we wrestle with Him so we are not deceived. The enemy wants us to take our eyes off God, the only true source of comfort and healing. Just as the serpent tempted Eve in Genesis, the enemy often twists the word of God in a way that sounds nice, but leads us away from the truth and harms us in the end. He whispers, "Did God really say…?" *Does God really love you? Is God really good?*

I believe multiple factors can contribute to depression, such as chemical imbalances and complicated grief, and am a supporter of therapy, taking medication when needed, and seeking the support of professionals God has equipped and placed in our lives to help. While depression is not exclusively a spiritual issue, Satan doesn't play fair and would love to squeeze his way into our depression. He didn't look at me and say, "Kristin has already gone through a lot this year and her faith has already been shaken. She's already battling PTSD and depression, so I'll back off." No way. I can imagine him looking at me and saying, "Kristin is already at her lowest point. I'm going to do whatever I can to make sure she gives up any sliver of hope she still clings to."

As I wrestled with God, I battled feelings of loneliness, inadequacy, and hopelessness. I was often shaken awake in the middle of the night with intense nightmares, often of people dying in front of me, and was too afraid to fall back asleep. Nothing in my future seemed good, except for life after death with Jesus. I hid beneath the blankets and battled big, fat lies—fiery arrows from the enemy as he tried to take advantage of my pain and my doubts.

You're worthless. You couldn't even keep your baby alive. You're stupid. You cry too much.

You're ugly. Just look at your swollen belly and giant scar. Disgusting.

You are awkward to be around. No one likes you anymore. You failed your husband. He's going to find someone else who can give him a child.

The enemy had been planting lies in my mind and I had been accepting them. I had allowed the enemy to knock me down and destroy my hope. Even in my wrestling, I cried out to God for help. Even after all the angry words I had hurled at Him, I felt God whispering His truth to me. It did not come in an audible voice, but rather in the soft prompting of the Holy Spirit. *You don't have to fight this alone. Give it to me.* The tears continued to fall, but my breathing steadied.

The whole time I had been wrestling with God, a battle had been raging around me. I often forget the reality of spiritual warfare. I think many Christians in the Western world do. All of us are in the midst of a raging battle every day and rarely take the time to consider it. I had always believed that biblical depictions of God, Satan, angels, and demons were literal and true. I knew spiritual warfare is real, but I had rarely taken the time to consider its effect on me.

Each of us face spiritual warfare on a regular basis. The question is, are we prepared to fight back? As I searched the scriptures for truth, the reality of spiritual warfare was continually reinforced. In Ephesians 6:10–18, the apostle Paul talks about the battle we wage and the tools God has given us to counteract an attack:

> Finally, be strong in the Lord and in the strength of his might. Put on the whole armor of God, that you may be able to stand against the schemes of the devil. For we do not wrestle against flesh and blood, but against the rulers, against the authori-

ties, against the cosmic powers over this present darkness, against the spiritual forces of evil in the heavenly places. Therefore take up the whole armor of God, that you may be able to withstand in the evil day, and having done all, to stand firm. Stand therefore, having fastened on the belt of truth, and having put on the breastplate of righteousness, and as shoes for your feet, having put on the readiness given by the gospel of peace. In all circumstances take up the shield of faith, with which you can extinguish all the flaming darts of the evil one; and take the helmet of salvation, and the sword of the Spirit, which is the word of God, praying at all times in the Spirit, with all prayer and supplication.

Prayer, faith in Who God is even when we don't feel it, and the truth we find in God's Word are our weapons. A battle was taking place in my life and I needed to arm myself. I needed to cling to the truth, hold fast to my faith, dig deeper into the scriptures and pray constantly.

1 Peter 5:8–9 says, "Be sober minded; be watchful. Your adversary the devil prowls around like a roaring lion, seeking someone to devour. Resist him, firm in your faith, knowing that the same kinds of suffering are being experienced by your brotherhood around the world." The devil is not indifferent to us. He hates us and wants to destroy us. We must resist him and cling to our faith, even in the midst of intense suffering. Verse ten continues, "And after you have suffered a little while, the God of all grace, who has called you to his eternal glory in Christ, will himself restore, confirm, strengthen, and establish you." Battles are not usually won overnight. Typically, an army must fight

constantly for days, months, and sometimes even years before the battle is won. I quickly realized my battle with depression, like an earthly battle, was going to take time. My anxiety would keep me tethered to Jesus, constantly turning to Him to be my strength.

As I lay in bed and wrestle, I use the truth of God's word as my arsenal against the lies of the enemy.

I have been created in the image of God. (Genesis 1:27) I was knit together by God. I am fearfully and wonderfully made. (Psalm 139:13–15)

God knows me intimately. He knows how many hairs are on my head. (Luke 12:6–7)

God sent Jesus to die for me, even while I was still in my sin. (Romans 5:8)

I have been adopted. (Ephesians 1:5)

Nothing can separate me from the love of Christ. (Romans 8:37–39)

I am forgiven. (1 John 1:9)

I have been saved. (Romans 9:9–10)

As I wrestle, God remains good and faithful. As my heart breaks, he is near. We will face many afflictions, but God will deliver his children from them all. (Psalm 34:18–19)

I will face many troubles in this world, but I can breathe easy knowing Jesus has overcome the world. (John 16:33)

Twelve

All of it

I n the middle of our series of miscarriages, my husband was rushed to the emergency room. On Christmas Day. Early that morning, Chris had been complaining of chest pains. I coaxed him into stopping by the local urgent care before we dove headfirst into Christmas celebrations with our families. "Just to give us peace of mind," I said. One hour and an abnormal EKG later, an ambulance was rushing him to the nearest hospital.

I held it together until Chris was safely loaded into the ambulance before completely falling apart. I was terrified I was about to lose him too and the noises, smells, and sights of the hospital threatened to drag me back to the moment the medical team attempted to revive Ethan. I was crippled with fear. God had allowed Ethan to die and I had no reason to believe He wouldn't allow the same to happen to Chris.

I wasn't allowed to ride in the ambulance with Chris, so I followed in my car. I screamed and cried the whole way to the hospital. "GOD. Why?" I wailed, pounding my fist against the steering wheel. "Please, please don't take my husband from me. I trusted You with our infertility. I trusted You when Ethan was sick, and even after he died.

I trusted You when you took our second baby. And our third. GOD. I've trusted You through so much. What more do You want from me? *Haven't I proved to You that I trust You enough?*"

I didn't hear a clear voice and I didn't see a sign from heaven. There wasn't a billboard on the freeway or a song on the radio. But in that moment, I felt a peace wash over me and the Holy Spirit clearly pressed this message onto my heart.

Enough? Kristin, I want you to trust Me with all of it. Every single corner of your life. Trust Me with everything. Give Me all of it.

We do that, don't we? I know I did. We give God pieces of our lives and think we've done our duty. We say, "Here, God, take my possessions and my career, but don't touch my health. I trust You with my marriage, but not with my children. I give You my past, but let me determine my future. I give You my future, but let me cling to my past."

In refusing to surrender certain pieces of my life to God, did I truly trust Him? Even if I had trusted Him with 95 percent of my life, could I truly say I trusted Him if I was clinging to the other 5 percent? If I believe God is Who He says He is—that He is good, loving, just, perfect, infinite, all-powerful, merciful, holy, almighty, I AM, faithful—I need to trust Him with every piece of my life. If I withhold even just one piece from Him, am I truly believing He is everything He says He is? I was holding what felt like one of the only precious things I had on earth—my husband—tightly in my grip. God wanted me to surrender and trust Him with my marriage too.

To make a long story short, the issue turned out to be minor and the doctors felt confident sending Chris home after several days of tests and exams. I was incredibly thankful and cried tears of relief when doctors declared his heart healthy.

This experience feels small in comparison to the difficulties we had faced that year, but it challenged me to consider how much I truly trusted God. It's easy to encourage others to put their trust in Him when things begin to fall apart. The words roll off my tongue so effortlessly as I encourage others, but how much do I really, truly trust Him when the rubber meets the road and the unimaginable begins to unfold?

Losing Ethan challenged my trust in God. When the doctors told us our son may not survive, I knew God had a plan. Yes, I was afraid. Yes, my heart was filled with questions. In spite of the fear, I knew God is sovereign. After years of unexplained infertility, we had miraculously conceived and I saw God's hand in every aspect of Ethan's existence. Despite my absent menstrual cycles and taking a break from "trying", he was given to us. Despite my fears, I trusted God was intricately forming each piece of Ethan's body and held each heartbeat in His hands. I knew God is sovereign in both life and death. As Ethan breathed his last breath, cradled in our arms, my broken heart knew God was sovereign in each of the ninety-three minutes our son was on this earth and would continue to be sovereign as we grappled with his death. I am not saying it was easy, but deep down I *knew* it.

It may be easy to assume I was completely placing my trust in God. I even fooled myself. Our journey with Ethan strengthened my trust in God, but I still held corners of my life with a tight grip. If we're honest, I think many of us find ourselves there. We fully surrender certain areas of our lives while clinging fiercely to other precious pieces.

I realized I was clinging to the other 5 percent. By doing so, I was asserting I could handle my life better than God could. I was implying God was not trustworthy enough to hold my entire life in His hands. The realization was sobering. Sometimes trust grows through kicking, screaming, and wrestling—there was a lot of that. My trust grew in that season of wrestling and pain.

Haven't I trusted You enough? Part of the problem lies in the question itself. In putting perimeters on trust, I was implying God could only be trusted with specific parts of my life. I was implying other areas of my life were mine, not His. I've been challenged to consider what areas of my life aren't included in the "enough". What areas am I clinging to that I don't want to let go?

If we are honest with ourselves, I'd guess many of us have those corners of our lives we don't want to let go of. For me those areas had been my infertility. Our children. My health. I had watched each of those things be pried from my fingers and I desperately clung to all I felt I had left. I was desperate to remain in control. All the while, Jesus was calling out to me to cling to Him instead. All the while, God lovingly beckons us, "*I want you to trust Me with all of it.*"

I started to chronicle our story about a month after Ethan died. Writing was an outlet for me. I sat at home all day in a house with closed blinds, heavy with sorrow and depression. I was so tired. My heart was tired. My body was tired. Despite how our story had wrecked me, I did not want to forget any of it. I wanted to record each moment while it was fresh. As my fingers danced across the keyboard and the words began to fill the screen, God began to pour His peace upon me. He began to show me the ways He was woven into our story. Beyond that, He began to show me this isn't our story—this is His story.

As I poured out my heart into words, I contemplated how I would end the story I was writing. I hoped and prayed I'd become pregnant again. Perhaps another baby would be the redemption at the end of a heartbreaking story. That ending was the 5 percent I was clinging to. God could have the other 95 percent of my life.

I had reached what seemed like a dead end in writing out our story. For months, I stopped writing. I waited and waited for the happy ending to come. I waited for the rainbow after the storm. After five losses, I wasn't sure I should keep trying.

What if healing doesn't come? What if our dreams never unfold in the way we had once hoped? What if God has something different for our lives? Some of us may not receive "that thing" we always longed for and we cannot believe our lives are any less valuable because of it. "That thing," as good as it may be, will never fully satisfy us and is not our highest calling. Only Jesus holds that power.

There is nothing wrong with the so-called happy ending. I rejoice each time I hear that anyone—especially a barren womb or a sister-in-loss—is expecting a child. Children are a blessing. Fulfilled dreams are a blessing. My prayer for myself, and for those around me, was that these earthly desires would be fulfilled and our home would one day be filled with the sounds of children laughing (and yes, even screaming). But I began to loosen my grip on that last percent of my life I had clung to so dearly. It was possible God may never allow me to have more children and I wanted to completely trust Him with that.

The truth is, God is the redemption in our story. Even if I were to have multiple children, I would never find redemption through them. A new baby wouldn't redeem our story. A baby—God coming to earth through Jesus Christ—already has.

I was never promised an easy life. I was never promised a home filled with children. I was never promised a life without pain. I was never promised perfect health. I thought back to John 16:33 yet again. I was promised a struggle, but greater than that, I was promised God is greater than any struggle I may face.

I often think about what Debbie told me—no matter what happens, God will never leave you empty-handed. This is the truth I need to cling tightly to when I feel discouraged. Not an empty promise that my fickle dreams will all unfold, but a firm promise you and I can stand on. No matter what happens—suffering, loss, abandonment, disappointment, despair—God will never leave us empty-handed.

In all reality, we may lose everything in this life. Our plans may never unfold in the way we once expected them to. I often need to be reminded that in this world, I may have nothing—but if I have Christ, I have everything.

"I just feel so out of control," I said to Chris one night as we were cleaning the kitchen after dinner.

Chris stopped what he was doing and said something so wise and so encouraging—something I've always known, but wasn't truly grasping before that moment. I think of it often.

"We've always been out of control—we just realize it now."

With each passing day, God has continued to remind me of just how much He is in control and just how little I am in control, and it has been comforting to rest in that truth. I knew it would be okay if our plans fell apart. Our worth rested in Jesus, not in our best-laid plans. I wanted to lay my plans at His feet. I wanted to give Him all of it.

Thirteen

So why pray?

N early two months after losing our identical twins, I became pregnant with our sixth child. Every-thing was textbook normal until my body unex-pectedly went into labor at only twenty-two weeks gestation. I found myself on hospital bedrest, desperately trying to keep my baby inside of me. Everything in me wanted to cry out to God to have mercy on me, but I felt too weary with disappointment and feelings of betrayal. I had already spent countless hours begging God to spare the five babies who had come before, and He had chosen to heal them eternally rather than physically. Every time I opened my mouth to pray, there were no words left. I was paralyzed by fear.

I spent the next two and a half months in the hospital, asking God to help me believe He hears my prayers even if He says no. I asked Him to help me believe He had the power to protect the child in my womb, who I thought I would lose. I didn't know how to pray and, thankfully, God is powerful enough to act without my prayers. This time, God chose to say yes. Our precious miracle boy "A" was born healthy at thirty-two weeks and I wept with joy at his birth. Today I weep with gratitude when I consider the gift of his life and the incredible generosity God showed me in allowing my husband and me to parent him on earth. I love that kid more than words can say.

Since his miraculous birth and each incredible milestone, I have often found myself asking the question "What is the point of prayer?" I was cautious to admit my wrestling with this question because I didn't want God or anyone else to think I was anything but grateful. Yet I wrestled as I attempted to reconcile why God said no to years of pleading and yes when I had little words to offer. (Spoiler alert: I believe it has everything to do with His sovereign plan and very little to do with my words.)

It has been helpful for me to first take a step back and define what prayer is and what it is not. Somewhere along the line, culture, media, and my own experiences shaped my perception of prayer. Prayer doesn't require specific words or a specific language. Prayer is simply talking to God. It is not just asking God for things, but it can also include thanksgiving, praise, repentance, and even grief and lament.

In my study, the simplest answer I have found to the "why pray" question is that God asks us to. Scripture is filled with instructions to pray (Matthew 6:5–15, Romans 12:12, Ephesians 6:18, Philippians 4:6, 1 Thessalonians 5:17, 1 Timothy 2:1, and James 5:14, just to name a few examples.) Second, we pray because we *can*. Prayer is something we often take for granted. There was a time when we didn't have the privilege to converse so freely with God and we *get* to because of Jesus. Hebrews 4:16 says, "Let us then with confidence draw near to the throne of grace, that we may receive mercy and find grace to help in time of need." The word confidence means being able to speak freely without fear or shame. We no longer need to go through a priest or walk through a list of rituals to communicate with God. Jesus is now our high priest, who made a way for us to approach God as our Father.

Earthly miracles, whether those of Jesus in the New Testament or those God does today, give us a glimpse of how our world was created to be before sin and brokenness entered it. Miracles also give us a glimpse into a future of restoration—when Jesus returns and every tear is wiped from our eyes and the new heavens and the new earth are established. In addition to pointing us toward Eden and future glory, Jesus used miracles to authenticate his divinity and to prove He was who He said He was. Many people believed and followed Him based on miracles He performed, culminating with the ultimate miracle of the resurrection.

While I do believe God can do miracles today, He already did the only miracle that truly sustains us for eternity, which is providing a way for us to be reconciled to Him based solely on grace alone. God didn't owe us that, nor does he owe us anything above that, yet Hebrews tells us we can boldly approach the throne of God with confidence knowing He hears us and loves us. Praise God that He doesn't rely on the fervency of my prayers to accomplish His will. No number of earthly miracles can take away our need for Him, nor can any amount of earthly suffering or brokenness separate us from His love and faithful promises.

Jesus perfectly models prayer throughout the gospels and I have been particularly encouraged by His words in the Garden of Gethsemane, just before He was turned over to be crucified. Jesus—God in human likeness—knew the horrific death He would die, the separation He would experience from the Father when He took on our sin, and that He would rise again, conquer death, and be restored with the Father. Even with this knowledge, Jesus' soul was "overwhelmed with sorrow to the point of death" (Matthew 26:38) when He considered what was coming. He knew the victorious ending, yet He was distressed to the point of sweating droplets of blood as He pleaded with the Father to provide another avenue for the salvation of His children to be accomplished. Yet in His very next breath, He submitted to the will of the Father. "Not as I will, but as you will." In other words, "I trust what you have decided."

We have the freedom to humbly ask our all-powerful and sovereign Father for miracles, for physical healing, and for earthly restoration. We can ask, fully knowing and trusting God has the power to do this, just as Jesus did. Yet I believe our prayers should be built upon the humble submission displayed by Christ: "Not my will, but yours be done." I want those words to dominate my prayers. I want to spend the bulk of my time seeking God's glory and asking Him to carry out His will in my life and in the lives of those around me.

I've spent hours wrestling through scriptures like Matthew 7:7–8, where Jesus tells his disciples to "ask, and it will be given to you." Upon further study, I have found that Jesus is often referring to spiritual healing and spiritual gifts—things that bring Him glory and will not fade. The women's ministry at my church recently participated in an inductive study on 1 John. Each week, I gathered with a small group of women on a friend's back patio as we dove deeper into the text line by line. As we reached 1 John 3, I found myself bristling as we read the words in verse 22, "And whatever we ask we receive from him, because we keep his commandments and do what pleases him." I shared my struggle with the women in my small group and we wrestled through the words together, stepped back to look at the greater context, and ultimately landed on this: the prayers referred to would not be for worldly priorities and personal gain, but for what pleases God. When we are transformed by the Holy Spirit, our desires shift to align with God's heart and a desire to bring Him glory.

Perhaps I have bristled at scriptures like this because of the way the message of the "prosperity gospel"—that affluence, health, and an easy life are the result of following Jesus—has crept into our culture. Phrases like "Follow Jesus and life will be easy" or "Have enough faith and Jesus will heal you" contradict the teachings of Jesus. The prosperity gospel is a false gospel. Jesus guarantees struggles for His children and assures us we will face trials. He reminds us that the poor, the mourning, and the meek are blessed. He promises us an even greater gift than wealth, physical health, or status. He promises us salvation and eternal life with Him.

I heard a lot of prosperity-driven statements when we learned of Ethan's prognosis. Things like "God is going to heal him because of your faith." These words troubled me because they didn't line up with the experiences of those around me and, even more importantly, they didn't line up with scripture. While God invites us to come to Him with confidence, He does not choose to answer our prayers based on the number of hours we spend on our knees or how much sweat forms on our brow when we talk to Him. He isn't holding a scale, waiting for our prayers to heap up on one side, causing it to tip in our favor. God doesn't need our prayers to act. He is infinitely bigger than this and we cannot mess up His plan by not praying "hard enough" or not having enough faith. Sure, we can miss out on the blessing of communing with Him and the way He draws near and transforms our hearts when we pray, but we can't screw up His good plan. The prayer of faith isn't certain God will provide us with the specific earthly thing we ask for, but rather it is certain of Who God is. It is certain of His character, His power, and that He hears us. The prayer of faith is confident yet submissive. It rests in the goodness of God, even when the details don't make any sense in our eyes.

I am grateful for the ability to approach God and converse with Him. I am grateful He hears. I am also grateful He doesn't *need* me to carry out His will. I'm grateful the outcome does not rest on my shoulders and on my eloquent words (or lack thereof). I'm grateful when I don't have the words to pray the Holy Spirit speaks on my behalf. Romans 8:26 says, "Likewise the Spirit helps us in our weakness. For we do not know what to pray for as we ought, but the Spirit himself intercedes for us with groanings too deep for words."

Kristin Hernandez

Fourteen

Why did God let my babies die?

*I*f there is a good God, why is there so much suffering
in the world? I've heard this question countless times
and it's something I too have asked. I didn't understand how a good God could allow an innocent child to
die. It didn't add up that we had repeatedly lost babies
when we had pursued pregnancy with so much prayer.
I couldn't see how God could allow us to lose so much
when our desire had been to honor God with our family.
It made me angry.

In the midst of the unthinkable, I was seeking the root
cause. I think most of us have an inner drive to explain
why painful things happen because it gives us an illusion
of being in control, and control is undeniably comfortable.
Cancer? "It was probably because of exposure to chemicals."
Lost their house? "They were probably unwise with finances."
Multiple miscarriages? "Too much stress? Maybe cut out
gluten?" I looked for the source behind painful, sometimes
unexplainable things, and desperately tried to protect
myself and my family by avoiding anything that might

trigger these outcomes. *Innocent babies die?* I couldn't even begin to imagine a reason.

I wrestled with wondering if my own actions had led to the death of my children. What if I had seen the signs sooner? What if I had selected a different hospital? Had I done something wrong? Was God angry at me?

I believe there are consequences for our sin. Sure, it is possible for suffering to be the fallout from poor choices or evil acts committed by mankind. There are biblical examples of God disciplining His children and, in reality, we all deserve death. This is what makes the death and resurrection of Jesus and the redemption we can have in Him so beautiful. He bore our shame and our punishment. While some of the suffering I saw around me was the direct result of poor choices, most of it appeared to be random. People who lived in opposition to God had easy, fun-filled lives and people who had devoted their lives to Christ and to serving their neighbors were afflicted with unthinkable pain.

I held a transactional view of God's goodness toward us. I believed good things happen to good people and that He would give me a comfortable life if I followed all of the right steps. I had subconsciously bought the lie that all suffering was a direct consequence of disobedience. You sinned and God punished you. You were "good" and God rewarded you with a life of ease. In my human eyes, this view seemed straightforward and fair. As I opened my Bible and read from God's word, I began to see my view was completely missing the mark.

A beautiful story in John 9 brings me comfort and frees me of shame. Jesus' disciples encounter a man who has been blind since birth. They ask Jesus, "Rabbi, who sinned, this man or his parents, that he was born blind?" I have found myself asking similar questions. Jesus, who sinned, me or my husband, that our son was born with Trisomy 9? Jesus, is it the sin of my past or the idols of my heart that caused me to miscarry our children? Jesus' response shatters the transactional assumptions many of us hold. "It was not that this man sinned, or his parents, but that the works of God might be displayed in him." Jesus doesn't waste tragedy. While Jesus weeps with us in our sorrow and stands as the ultimate enemy of death, He is bigger than our decisions and bigger than our mistakes. He is sovereign over everything. He uses all things, even the most painful things we can imagine, for our good and for His glory.

When we take our very real and often valid emotions as truth, we will ultimately be led astray. When we're faced with difficult questions such as this, it's important that we turn to scripture. We need to cling to the truth of the Bible, even when (or especially when) the desire to read doesn't come naturally.

I once heard Pastor Tim Keller say we are one of the first cultures and generations to be surprised by pain and suffering, and my own observations lead me to agree. People have struggled and suffered since the beginning of time, many in ways I can hardly begin to grasp. In John 16:33, Jesus says, "In the world you will have tribulation. But take heart; I have overcome the world." Tribulation isn't just some awful thing that sneaks into our lives when we aren't looking—it is a promise. Jesus guaranteed we would suffer. He invites us to suffer with Him. But He doesn't stop there. There is an even greater promise—that He has already overcome the world and we can rest in this assurance.

A quote from Pastor David Rieke describes so well this guaranteed suffering and the hope we can cling to as we await relief. He said, "Life is truly and mostly a war. If we think life is mostly a delightful journey of some kind, then we will probably feel surprised and short-changed when bad things happen. But if life is mostly a war, then tears, pain, death, and deprivation are 'normal.' Until our side finally wins, we have USO shows, letters from home, talks with buddies, and heroic moments. Still, the journey of war is never mostly delightful."[4]

The battlefield is expected to be difficult. We wouldn't arrive on the front lines only to be shocked it wasn't a sunny vacation. In this same way, we can expect to face trouble in this world. We fight. We cry out. We lament. We hold fast to Jesus, using His Word as our weapon. We exhale with relief, knowing we don't need to wonder which side will win this war. Jesus has already won the battle.

Like care packages and wartime camaraderie, our earthly lives may bring pleasures in the midst of battle. God certainly gives good earthly gifts, such as our families, our friends, meaningful conversations, a beautiful sunset, and water to drink. These are good things and it is appropriate to respond with joy and gratitude. But the reality is, even these things will pass away. As we enjoy the good gifts God has given us earthside, we must establish our hearts in the kingdom of God. That is where our treasure should be. That is where our gaze should be set. That is what we are working toward. James 5:1–11 reminds me of this truth and admonishes me to remain patient in suffering. We are like farmers sowing seeds and patiently waiting for the harvest. We expectantly await the blessing of the harvest, often forgetting the truest blessing is the one we will have

---

4. Rieke, David. Avalon Hills Bible Church.

in Christ when He returns. When His kingdom comes to earth. When all comes to a glorious completion and all wrongs are made right.

This world is temporary. Our possessions will rot and our bodies will die. As the preacher in Ecclesiastes declares, "All is vanity." We work, we build, we die. Our lives are only a vapor, a tiny droplet of steam rising from a cup of coffee and vanishing into the air above, compared to the vast span of eternity. To those who don't know Jesus, these words are hopeless. The words lead to death, judgment, pain, and darkness. Separation from God. But for the one who believes in Jesus, there is an incredible hope beyond this despair.

James 5:10–11 says, "As an example of suffering and patience, brothers, take the prophets who spoke in the name of the Lord. Behold, we consider those blessed who remained steadfast. You have heard of the steadfastness of Job, and you have seen the purpose of the Lord, how the Lord is compassionate and merciful." As I walk through the minefields of suffering, I consider those who have gone before me. Joseph, who was sold by his brothers and spent more than twenty years in Egypt (including years in prison). David, who sinned against God and lost a newborn son. Job, who lost everything he had. These men didn't know the end of the story like we do yet they trusted God. Even with tears of lament and deep grief, they humbly worshipped the Lord and trusted Him to accomplish His will in their lives.

As I wrestle through the question of why God allows pain to enter our lives, I'm both encouraged and challenged by the story of Job, a righteous man who asked similar questions as he waded through unimaginable suffering. Shortly after we lost the twins, I purchased a twelve-week

Bible study guide that explored the theme of suffering in relationship to God's goodness and sovereignty. In this study, I dove deep into the book of Job for what felt like the first time. I had read the story of Job multiple times, but it had never truly left an impression on me until then.

Job was a righteous man who, although not perfect, was living a righteous life in line with God's will. His righteousness both pleased God and caught the eye of the evil one, Satan. One day, Satan approached God and said, "Job only praises you because his life is so good. He has riches, land, children, and good health. If you take those things away, Job would definitely turn his back on you" (paraphrased). God responded to this challenge by giving Satan permission to harass Job and take everything from him, except for his life.

Almost immediately, Job lost nearly everything dear to him, including his children, his livestock, and his health. Chapters 4–37 of the book of Job contain a dialogue between Job and the friends who came to "comfort" him. His friends were convinced Job's misfortune was a result of hidden sin and repeatedly urged Job to turn from his wicked ways and repent. Meanwhile, poor Job was at a complete loss as to what he had done to deserve such suffering. He cursed his own life and wished he had never been born. "I've searched my heart! If you know something I don't know, please tell me so I can repent," Job pleaded (again, paraphrasing). All the while, Job cried out for a Redeemer. He cried out for the coming Christ. "If only there were an advocate to stand in my place and argue my righteousness before the Father," he cried.

I love how even this passage points to the coming of the Messiah. Job cried out for an advocate to speak to God on his behalf and to make him righteous and we now have one because of Jesus! I am a sinner and deserve nothing but death. Someone had to die to make things right and just. Despite our wretchedness, Jesus died in our place so we could be seen as righteous before God. This blows my mind. After chapters and chapters of Job suffering, crying out to God to put him out of his misery, and receiving misplaced advice from well-meaning supporters (anyone else relate?), God finally spoke to Job in chapter 39. Rather than answer all of Job's questions or give a thorough explanation for his suffering, God simply told Job who *He* is. He asked Job, "Were you there when I created the earth and set the sun in its place?" He continued to list the magnificent, unimaginable things He had accomplished and asserted His sovereignty. He simply told Job of His own character and reminded Job of his own mortality and humanity in light of God's grandeur.

Job's response in chapter 42 has left a deep imprint on my broken heart, as I have wrestled and explored this text. Verses 1–6 say:

> Then Job answered the Lord and said:
> "I know that you can do all things,
>   and that no purpose of yours can be thwarted.
> 'Who is this that hides counsel without
>   knowledge?'
> Therefore I have uttered what I did not
>   understand,
>   things too wonderful for me, which I did
>   not know.
> 'Hear, and I will speak;
>   I will question you, and you make it known
>   to me.'

I had heard of you by the hearing of the ear,
but now my eye sees you;
therefore I despise myself,
and repent in dust and ashes."

I'm not sure I'll ever know why God allowed Ethan and four of our other children to die. When I reflect on the majesty and the goodness of God, my need for a specific answer fades away. Like Job, I begin to recognize that I have all the answers I need when I meditate on Who God is and all He has done. When I stand before God one day, my suffering will be of no concern to me. I will be so swept up in awe of Him that every bit of excruciating pain I have ever experienced will feel light and insignificant in comparison to the treasure I have in Him.

Like Job, we come face to face with our own smallness when we suffer. Our trials have a way of drawing us to Christ. Our tribulations open our eyes and ears to see and hear Him. Our pain loosens our grip on what is temporary and points us toward what is eternal. It reveals our need for Jesus to be our advocate, to stand in the gap and allow us to enter into a relationship with our great Father.

Suffering is a guarantee for those who follow Jesus. I grew up believing the opposite of this to be true. "Go to church and your family will be happy. Don't have sex before marriage and God will give you healthy children. Trust God and everything will come easy to you." While God certainly calls us to draw near to Him and walk in holiness, He isn't a vending machine. The idea is incredibly unpopular and uncomfortable, but Jesus promised us we would struggle (John 16:33). I was never promised a pain-free life. I was never promised an easy road to travel. I was never promised perfect health, a perfect marriage, three healthy children, and financial security. What you and I are promised is suffering—and that God would never leave us or forsake us through any of it. We have been promised the opportunity to experience salvation, deliverance, and an eternity with Jesus. We have been promised something much better than an easy life.

The promises of a hard life are found throughout scripture. In Matthew 7:14, Jesus says that the gate is narrow and the way that leads to life is hard. He adds, "Those who find it are few." Following Jesus is not easy and He warned us of that. In Luke 9:23–25, Jesus says, "If anyone would come after me, let him deny himself and take up his cross daily and follow me. For whoever would save his life will lose it, but whoever loses his life for my sake will save it. For what does it profit a man if he gains the whole world and loses or forfeits himself?" To many of us, the cross is a sign of comfort we often display in our homes or wear as jewelry. In the time in which Jesus spoke these words, the cross was a method of torment and execution. When Jesus says to take up our cross, He is basically telling us to take up our torture instrument and follow Him. He is warning us the road will not be easy and we will lose ourselves in the process.

Although there is the promise of pain, there is also the promise of hope. In John 16:33b, Jesus says to His disciples, "In the world you will have tribulation. But take heart; I have overcome the world." Suffering may be guaranteed, but so is the victory of Jesus Christ. Jesus came to die in our place, to take our shame so that we may be blameless before God, and to overcome death and shame for all time. He has overcome the most violent trials.

Approximately one thousand years before Jesus was born (give or take some years), David wrote in Psalm 34:19, "Many are the afflictions of the righteous, but the Lord delivers him out of them all." At times it may feel as if the word "many" doesn't even capture the onslaught of the pain and trials that have come our way, yet as I have studied scripture I have seen that scores of men and women in the Bible faced trials much larger and much more frequent than mine. Regardless of the type of trial or the frequency of the pain, I have found it comforting to see how God has truly delivered us from every single one of the many promised trials His children have faced—myself included.

Suffering has been one of the most horrible yet most precious gifts I have ever been given. Sometimes I wish I could go back to who I was before things got hard. I wish I could go back to the girl I was before struggling to conceive, before watching our long-awaited child die in our arms, and before miscarrying our second and our third and our fourth and fifth. But despite all of this, I would never want to trade the intimacy with Jesus I found when I was at my most broken. I would never want to give up the ways He has sanctified me and drawn me to Him in my pain. It is in my suffering I have felt the closest to Jesus. It is where I have seen the world for what it is—a broken place desperately in need of a savior. It is where I have finally seen heaven for the promise it is. It is through my suffering I have seen Jesus for the gift He is to a world of hurting hearts. Strangely, it is in my suffering I have found the most joy, the most good, and the most hope, intermingled with the pain.

I have begun to catch a glimpse of what Paul says in Philippians 3:8–11:

Indeed, I count everything as loss because of the surpassing worth of knowing Christ Jesus my Lord. For his sake I have suffered the loss of all things and count them as rubbish, in order that I may gain Christ and be found in him, not having a righteousness of my own that comes from the law, but that which comes through faith in Christ, the righteousness from God that depends on faith—that I may know him and the power of his resurrection, and may share his sufferings, becoming like him in his death, that by any means possible I may attain the resurrection from the dead.

Nothing in this world compares to the hope I have found in Jesus Christ. In this life, we may lose everything dear to us. We may suffer unthinkable pain. No matter what we go through, He understands our pain. He has invited us to share in His sufferings and in the power of His resurrection.

In Romans 5:3–5, Paul says, "Not only that, but we rejoice in our sufferings, knowing that suffering produces endurance, and endurance produces character, and character produces hope, and hope does not put us to shame, because God's love has been poured into our hearts through the Holy Spirit who has been given to us." It is extremely difficult to rejoice when everything is falling apart. In the hardest moments, rejoicing has been the furthest thing from my mind. When the pain has felt the most intense is when I have felt the least like praising God or giving thanks. Looking back, I have seen the endurance, character, and hope our trials have produced. My heart, although broken, has been filled with hope and I cannot help but rejoice in that.

The death of our son was horrific. The depression and anxiety I fight against is dreadful. The recurrent miscarriages and the toll each took on my body were terrible. The nightmares that have afflicted me are awful. God knows this. He knows this and He sent Jesus to restore all of the hurt, the shame, and the pain. It is through our suffering God has begun to chisel away at my rough edges and refine me to become more like Him. It does not make the bad things good—but it brings me such comfort to know God has remained both sovereign and good in every single detail. Nothing is beyond His redemption.

The Light shines in the darkness and the darkness has not overcome it (John 1:5). This is the light I cling to in the coldest darkness. The hope I cling to when questions, confusion, and doubt whirl around me like harsh winter winds. My life raft when the rain plummets down and the flash flood of despair attempts to drag me away with it. This is the hope I have in Christ.

The New Living Translation of 2 Corinthians 4:16–18 says, "That is why we never give up. Though our bodies are dying, our spirits are being renewed every day. For our present troubles are quite small and won't last very long. Yet they produce for us an immeasurably great glory that will last forever! So we don't look at the troubles we can see right now; rather, we look forward to what we have not yet seen. For the troubles we see will soon be over, but the joys to come will last forever." As I ponder why God allows suffering, this passage gives me perspective to view my pain through the lens of an eternity of joy with Jesus.

We have an assurance that this pain is not the end. We have the promise of His coming again. Even when the winds howl, the earth is barren, and the world feels so cold, the Son continues to shine. Wrestle with Him. Cry out to Him. Draw near to Him. Cling to Him. Rest in Him. There is joy coming. Hold on tight.

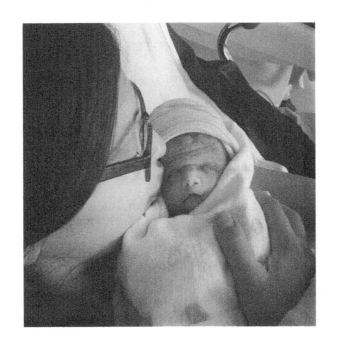

In loving memory of
Ethan Daniel Hernandez
August 16, 2015
1:32 p.m.– 3:05 p.m.

Endnotes

1. C.S. Lewis. *A Grief Observed*. (New York: Harper Collins, 1961), 10.

2. Greig, Pete. *God on Mute: Engaging the Silence of Unanswered Prayer*. (Grand Rapids: Baker Books, 2007), 202.

3. Ryan, Travis. You Hold It All. Integrity Music, 2015, Accessed April 4, 2021. https://open.spotify.com/ album/5amuOHLU6V7ktXtq3Apl4c

4. Rieke, David. Avalon Hills Bible Church.

Contact

Kristin Hernandez writes online at
sunlightindecember.com.

Email: sunlightindecember@gmail.com
Facebook: /sunlightindecemberblog
Instagram: @sunlightindecember

Made in the USA
Middletown, DE
20 March 2022

62778009R00089